ALL POWER IS GIVEN UNTO YOU

ELINOR S. MOODY

All Power is Given Unto You
by Elinor S. Moody

© Copyright 2021 Editorial RENUEVO, LLC.

All rights reserved.

No part of this publication may be reproduced, in whole or in part, stored in a retrieval system, or transmitted in any form or by any means – electronic, mechanical, digital, photocopy, recording or any other – without prior written permission of the publisher.

ISBN: 978-1-64142-226-0

Published by
Editorial RENUEVO LLC
www.EditorialRenuevo.com
info@EditorialRenuevo.com

Table of Contents

All Power is Given Unto You

Table of Contents

Chapter 1   9
Your Creative Mind

Chapter 2   21
How to Use Your Creative Mind

Chapter 3   35
All Power is Given Unto You

Chapter 4   43
The Secret of Success

Chapter 5   59
How to Concentrate

Chapter 6   75
Creative Power of the Word

Chapter 7   87
How to Use the Creative Power

Chapter 8   99
How to Speak the Creative Word

Chapter 9   111
Your Mind Dynamo

Chapter 10   123
As Ye Sow

Chapter 11   135
How to Direct the Mind Dynamo

Chapter 12   147
How to Create and Attract Your Own

All Power is Given Unto You

Chapter 1

Your Creative Mind

All Power is Given Unto You

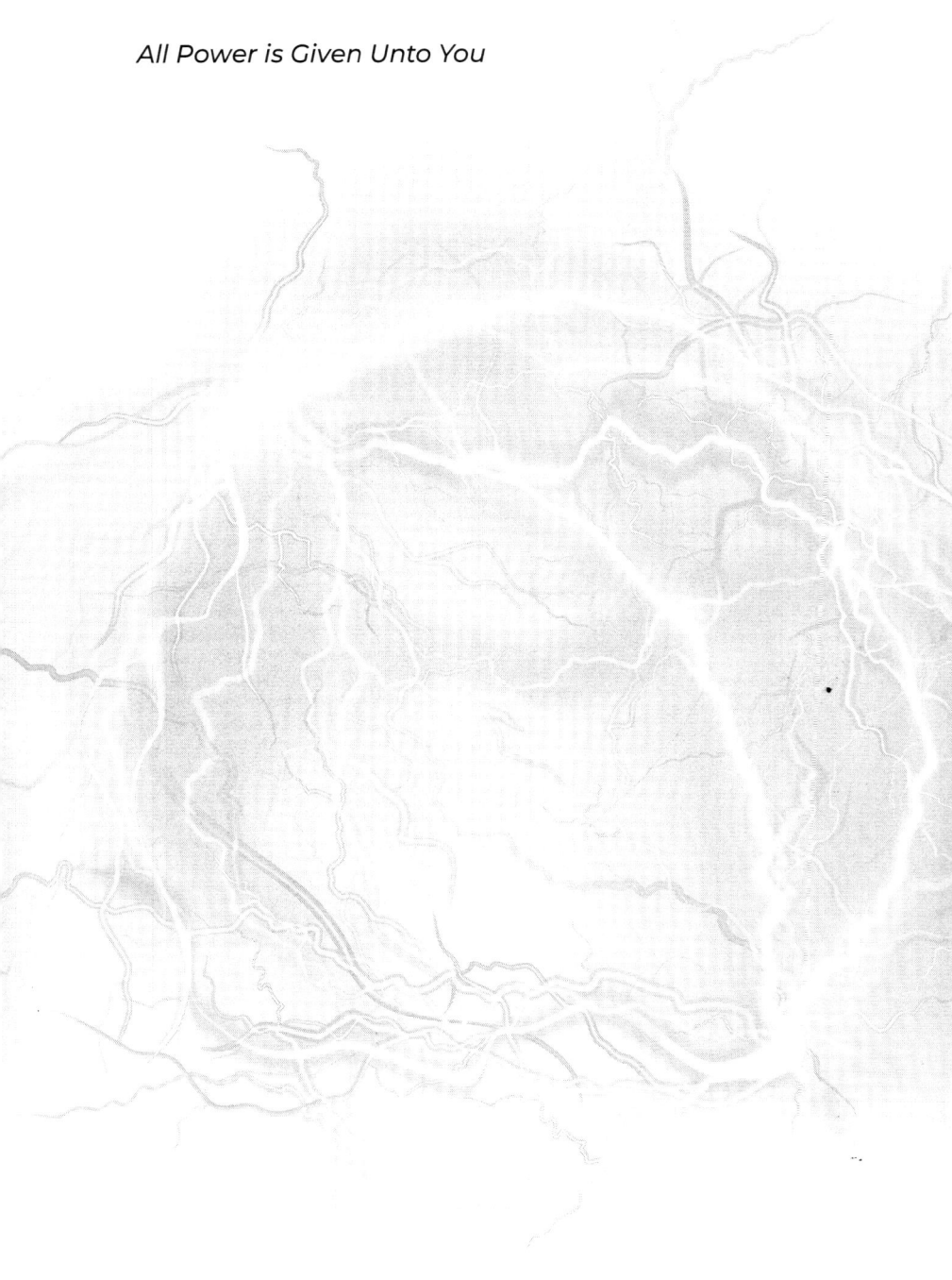

Your Creative Mind - 1

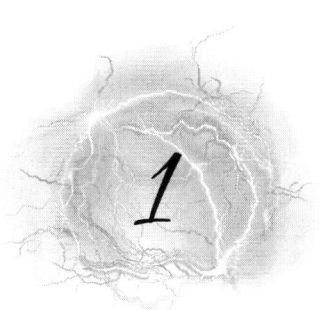

THE mind is the realm or workshop from which all things proceed, and in due time become visible to the eyes or senses.

This workshop is always open and ready for business, making quick use of whatever material we provide. Thus it is up to us, as individuals, to live lives of satisfaction, or the reverse.

But this is more than a matter of knowing how. To be sure, we must know how, but after that, we must steadfastly determine to live that knowledge constantly and consistently.

Happy, contented and optimistic thoughts soon crystallize into similar conditions in our lives, while unhappy, discouraged and discontented thoughts just as surely and naturally create after their kind.

And so have we, each one of us, created for ourselves the conditions in the midst of which we are this day living, whether those conditions are in accord with our desires or otherwise.

We are our own creators, and may create for ourselves whatsoever we desire. But let us remember that the things we create, whether by faith and trust or fear and doubt, are ours; and our own will come to us and will not go to another.

Nor can the things and conditions we create for ourselves be taken from us, until they have served their purpose in our lives and we are ready to pass them on, and replace them by something better for which we have daily been making ready.

Our own does not mean solely the things and conditions we desire, but rather the things upon which we fix the mind; the things with which we mentally relate ourselves, and by this mental relation create and in due season attract into visibility.

Thus, if we feed the mind with fear, doubt and worry thoughts, we are just as surely creating the things and conditions we think about as will be the case when we follow Paul's advice and think on the things of virtue and good report.

> As we think so we are, or so we shall create for ourselves; and the things and conditions we so create will naturally make themselves visible in and about us.

By fixing the conscious mind on a thing desired, or by allowing it to remain fixed on anything not desired, we shall impress that thing or condition on the inner, or so-called subconscious, mind. And in due season the inner mind will discover a way to express that thing in our lives in a perfectly natural manner, for there is very little of the supernatural in life.

When we begin to "think on these things," diligently and with the intent to understand the meaning of life, we find it very largely a matter of cause and effect—God, the All Good, being the first great cause of all life.

Mind is the pattern by which the word creates, for before we speak into being the thing or condition which brings to us pleasure or pain, we have either consciously or unconsciously been fashioning that thing or condition in the mental workshop, have been impressing, as it were, this pattern on the creative substance within and all about us. And it must come into sight, either in our acts or words, both of which express or objectify our thought children.

In this way do our thoughts build themselves into

our personalities, and so become what we appear to be.

As Matthew says, "The light of the body is the eye"; and we shall observe, in most instances, that the eye is a rather accurate indicator of the development of the inner power of understanding. As the power of thought is cultivated and controlled, the eye lights up with the glow of satisfaction, confidence and harmony; while the eye of the non-thinker, who is content to plod along today in the path of yesterday, not altogether satisfied, perhaps, but without any definite idea of changing conditions, will indicate a lack of that inner energy or fire which would so quickly and surely light up the inner realm or workshop and produce the "outward or visible signs."

The inner mind does its work with the utmost precision, faithfully producing or expressing all impressions made upon it by the outer or conscious mind, but of course it cannot express something that has not been given it by the outer mind. This is true even to the matter of building the face and figure in accord with the pattern provided by the conscious mind. This is worth remembering to those of us who would like to try re-constructing the physical self—the personality. And it is a fact that we can rebuild ourselves in accord with the most perfect physical pattern we are able to steadfastly and expectantly hold before the subconscious or inner mind.

In thinking of the inner and outer, or conscious and subconscious minds, let us not think of them as separate minds—or as two minds; for such is not the truth and it is only the truth that will make us really free. There is but the one mind and we are all individual parts of that great whole, just as the fingers are parts of the hand and the nails parts of the fingers. To discuss the mind in any other way is misleading, and seems to add a good deal of mystery to the simple and natural working of the mental mechanism.

The outer and inner phases of mind are only seemingly separate and distinct; just as the action of the fingers is seemingly separate and distinct from the action of the wrist and arm. It is the oneness of action in each case that makes for real value, and while the outer or conscious mind ceases its action when we sleep, the inner or subconscious does not cease its action at that time. But when the outer mind becomes somewhat befogged and out of normal condition, the inner mind likewise seems to have somewhat suspended its operation, since it needs the impression of the conscious mind in order that it may express the things and conditions desired or mentally considered.

We have to get the impression before we can put forth, or cause to become visible, the expression.

And even after what we have called the inner or

subconscious mind, science tells us there are still greater mental possibilities—that of the so-called super-conscious, of which I shall not speak here, since, for the purposes of this lesson, we shall do well to center our attention upon the natural working of the conscious and subconscious phases of mind alone.

Students of this subject tell us that the so-called subconscious realm is unlimited in its possibilities; that its storehouse of knowledge cannot be exhausted; that it holds the key to every problem and condition, and that when we have trained ourselves to turn to it quickly and confidently in time of need, it will always more than meet our expectation.

But do we do this, habitually? Or do we much more frequently entirely disregard this mental treasure house and go about declaring our inability to accomplish the thing desired? On excellent authority we have this declaration: "As a man thinketh in his heart, so is he."

The answer to our problem is always within, if we will search for it. If we will first think so, and then call confidently upon this great inner source of all knowledge to supply us with the needed ideas and ability.

If each one of us would learn, at all times, to confidently call upon the great inner source

Your Creative Mind - 1

of supply, expecting to receive the assistance sought, no life need be one of failures; for with this inner mind all things are possible, when we learn to rely upon it.

The conscious idea, or the information in sight at the moment, is as nothing compared to the inexhaustible supply which is always within, simply waiting to be recognized and called into action. And to this limitless supply we are constantly adding; though much of the time it may be done unconsciously.

But all this information that comes to us in the various ways, and of so much of which we are practically unconscious, duly classifies itself and produces fruit after its kind; whether it be to our satisfaction or otherwise. All the trifles over which we worry and fret are duly impressed upon this great inner field of consciousness, and are likely to express in our lives if we give them space in which to grow and come to maturity.

Right at hand, within ourselves, is "all that we can ask, or even think," in the way of help, if we will only learn to believe in it and receive of it. We need to think as to the meaning of that strong and simple promise, "Ask and ye shall receive." And if our asking is aright, failure is impossible.

Here is another interesting fact: The great inner storehouse of all knowledge uses the physical eye as a sort of advertising medium, and as one becomes accustomed to looking within for his or her supply of knowledge, the eye becomes constantly more indicative of the limitless power shining through it. It is interesting, as well as enlightening, to note the difference in degree of character indicated upon the faces of the men and women with whom we mix and mingle each day.

Regardless of the scope of the inner mind, it takes note of the minutest message sent it by the outer or conscious mind, and unerringly produces the thing or condition it is impressed to do. We must, however, furnish it with a pattern by which to work, or much of its remarkable power and ability will be lost to us, as is steam, gas or electricity when allowed to operate without careful direction, or for a specific purpose.

If we would constantly profit by the limitless power of this great inner realm, we must know just what we desire; must have a purpose in life. We must be ready to use the things and conditions desired; must know how to concentrate our thought force for good; must be able to mentally sketch or draw the thing or condition we desire to attract to ourselves.

Having passed such a pattern to the inner or subconscious realm or workshop, we may cease all doubts and fears and expectantly await the arrival of our own—the thing or condition we have created for ourselves and which is ours.

The inner mind will provide a way to express for us the thing we have impressed upon it, even giving to us the good measure, pressed down and running over, Father has promised; and it will do the work for us in a perfectly natural manner—so natural, many times, that we almost doubt that our own has come to us, and set it down as merely a wonderful happening, quite apart from the workings of the Spirit within.

This means study, of course, for we must first know what the law is, and then we must learn how to consciously connect with the all power with certainty and confidence—both in ourselves and in it. But this is well worth while. We would hardly expect to reap a profitable harvest had we failed in performing the necessary work in promoting its growth.

By the same natural law we obtain the benefits of the kingdom of all good. We must earn the right to have them before we may expect our rewards. And by earning the right to them, I mean we must do as our Father has told us to do on each and every occasion; and we must be happy in the doing, for we shall find cheerful obedience means much when it comes to receiving our "good measure, pressed down, shaken together and running over."

But having made "straight the way," there is no end to the achievements and attainments to which we may look forward, with perfect confidence in the promise, "Before they call I will answer and send them the desires of their hearts."

The matter of obtaining the things and conditions we desire is always in our own hands. But it means work, and if any of us are deceiving ourselves with the idea that demonstrating whatsoever we will is only a matter of knowing the pass-word or countersign, we are on the wrong scent or road, and it will be profitable for us to stop right here and get a new start in accord with Christ's "My Father worketh hitherto, and I work."

Chapter 2

How to Use Your Creative Mind

All Power is Given Unto You

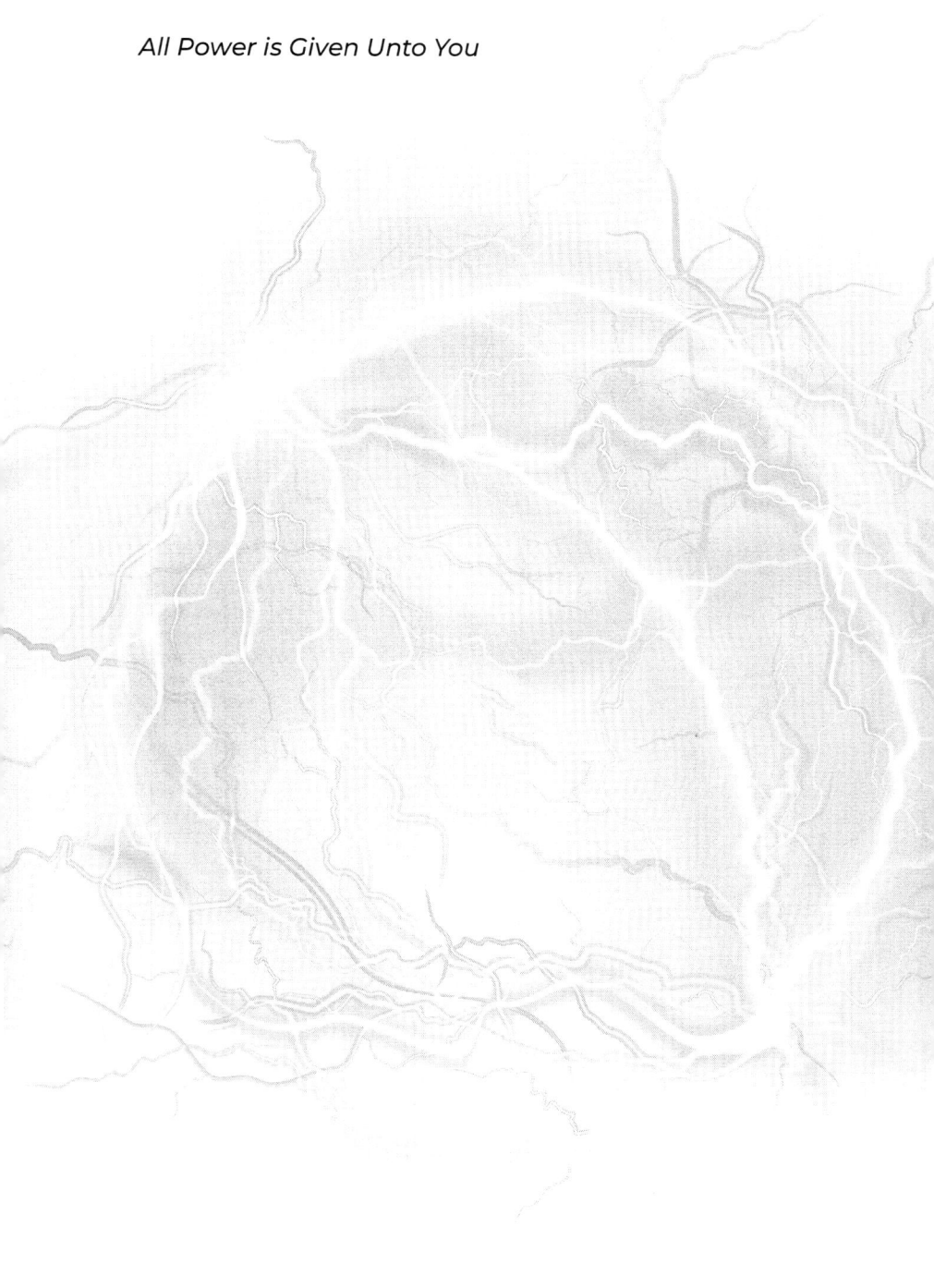

How to Use Your Creative Mind · 2

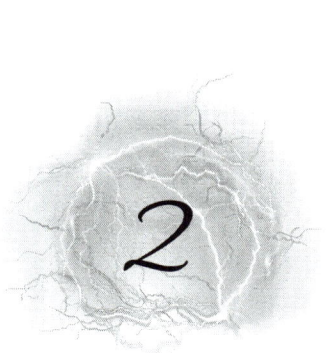

WHAT is the simple process of work in the matter of demonstration, or of attracting into visibility the things and conditions we desire? Shorn of unnecessary language, suppose we consider the simple, natural and workable manner of impressing the inner mind with the thing or condition it is desired to express—or to create and attract into visibility in our lives.

One of the first essentials in dealing with the subconscious mind, then, is to remember that its offices differ somewhat from the working of the conscious mind—or the outer portion of the mind, if that makes the matter easier for the present; that the mind is in every portion of the body or being, and not merely connected with the brain or "gray matter," as some of us have been encouraged to think. Some of our writers have likened the presence of the mind throughout the being as similar to the manner in which water saturates a sponge; and this is not a bad representation.

But it is important to remember that the subconscious mind is everywhere present in us, and that it is of a finer or more comprehensive quality than the outer or objective portion of the mind.

Subconscious means "lightly conscious: something taking place in the mind, without any attending consciousness, or conscious effort or perception," we are told; and this indicates how easily passing thoughts or events are photographed by this great inner camera.

We impress the inner mind directly through the thought or brain center, and by every sense of the body. This inner intelligence is in every portion of the make-up, and is ready at an instant's warning to come to our assistance when we invite it, and expect it to respond with its never failing ability.

The expectation is really an important part in the matter of results; for until we expect the assistance we invite or seek, we shall make no impression on the mind power within. And it cannot express what has not been impressed upon it by faithful conscious effort.

This is one reason, perhaps, why so much mental power goes to waste. We wish for things, but without the real expectation of obtaining them. And while the wish reaches the inner mind, because every thought or sense current passes to it, no impression is made on the within; and seldom will any result come from merely wishing for things or conditions, unless to the wishing is added the determined expectation of obtaining the thing desired.

But if this determined expectation is exercised, the great inner mind will always respond to our call, and we shall soon feel that a new and compelling power lives within us, which makes possible unto us all things, even the "exceeding, abundantly more" than we have yet asked for, or thought possible of attainment.

The inspiration of the Almighty opens our understanding to the truth that within us is unlimited power, with which we may at all times connect, if we are sufficiently in earnest to search for and obtain the key to this wonderful treasure house.

The meaning of this truth comes to us as intuition or inner knowledge at the moment when we desire to do a certain thing which seems to be quite unfamiliar to us, and which, perhaps, we have had the habit of thinking we were unable to do. If we call upon this great store of knowledge within, with confidence and honest expectation, we shall almost at once intuitively know that we can attain or achieve our purpose. Of course doubts, fears and uncertainties will have to be abandoned; but if we have faith in the work we are pursuing, negative ideas will begin to fall away of themselves without further effort on our part.

When we understand and accept the truth that all power is a part of us, is within us, as life, love, wisdom, knowledge, all and every good thing, we likewise understand that we are limitless, and that nothing can harm us or make us afraid. People and conditions which may have hitherto appeared to be all-powerful suddenly seem to have become powerless; while all our worries and misgivings take unto themselves wings and fly away, to return to us no more.

To believe actively that all power is within ourselves is the open road to the attainment of every desire the heart can know.

Often the question is asked, How may one arrive at that firm milestone of faith; and, having arrived, how may he make himself capable of staying there?

It is true, it is not always easy either to arrive or stay there after once arriving, until we really know in Whom we believe, and are persuaded that He is able to keep us as in the hollow of His hand, if we are in earnest in our purpose and willing to be kept.

One reason for slow progress in growing faith is that we let ourselves become discouraged over trifling obstacles, and so waste time and energy, which, if conserved, would take us a long way toward our desired goal of satisfaction. We only try these positive promises of Christ, wondering, as it were, if they really will work for us. And in this trying is the reason for our failure.

So long as we are experimenting with the promises of All Power, we are not stepping out on the "solid rock" of faith in God and His word, determined to sink or swim as He wills, as did Job, when he said, "Though He slay me, yet will I trust Him." It was at this period in Job's affairs that what some of us would call his "luck" changed, and he began to attract to himself good, and only good, whereas before this he had seemed to have plenty of trouble.

Universal Consciousness knows even the thoughts of our hearts, and so knows when we are positive in our work, and when we are otherwise; as was the man who came to Christ asking healing for his boy: "If You can do anything, have compassion on us, and help us" was his plea.

So frequently in seeking aid of Infinite Power, we indirectly invite it to prove to us that it can do what it has agreed to do. And if we seem to get sufficient proof or inspiration that it can and will shoulder our burdens, we then begin to talk about "holding the thought" in this or that way, that "all is coming out right"—right meaning really just as we would have it, in order that our purpose may be served, regardless of the other fellow who holds the opposite hand.

After "holding the thought" for some time, perhaps we discover no apparent change in affairs, and decide that so-called New Thought does not "work for us," and wonder why, when we know it does work for many others.

The answer to this question is that there is no reason why it should work for us. We have failed to do our mental work selflessly, and have been doing it selfishly, and therein is sufficient cause for defeat.

Let us get into Job's frame of mind and trust God regardless of self, and we shall soon find that New Thought works for us as well as for any other. Let us hold this thought to the exclusion of all others, and when we have impressed it upon the inner mind, we shall have no further cause for complaining of lack of desired results. It is believing in this inner portion of the all mind with which we are all connected, and taking advantage of the wonderful privileges it offers to us, that brings the freedom we so greatly desire—a satisfaction which may be broadened and deepened to whatever extent we are willing to think and work; for faith and works must always go hand in hand toward success.

When we realize that these mental gardens are our chiefest care, we shall not allow them to become "potters' fields," as it were, for the reception of any and every kind and condition of thought, since "As we sow (our thoughts), so shall we also reap." As we plant (or impress) the inner mind, thus will be the harvest ripening constantly in our lives.

If we are thinking and talking of poverty, illness and disharmony, the great within cannot take such seed and produce from it love, peace and plenty; for thought is the pattern in accord with which we shall create and speak into being the things about which we think and talk.

Let us remember that it is our own fault if we are poor, halt or blind. Those are the conditions we have impressed upon the inner mind, and it can only express what it has received in impression. It has to create in the unseen, according to the patterns we furnish.

The whole matter of demonstration or manifestation is in perfect accord with the Universal Law or the Gospel according to Christ; but which, perhaps, some of us have never well understood, even though we have read it over and over again.

For instance, He tells us to ask, believing that we do receive. But how often do we do this? How much more often do we make our asking so general that when we have finished we hardly know ourselves what we have desired of the Unseen.

To really impress the within, the inner mind, we should know exactly what we desire, in every particular, and we should then make a real business of centering our earnest thought—the conscious mind—upon this inner power, which is fully alive and conscious, even though we do not always have evidence of that consciousness.

It is the earnest thought that will impress upon the inner mind the desired thing or condition; and if we will free ourselves from all fears, doubts and worries as to receiving the desired good, it will in due season express, or come into visibility in our lives, in accord with Father's positive promise, "And if ye ask anything, believing in Me (that is, in My power and willingness to do all things, when you have asked aright), I will do it." There are things for us to do, and until we have done them we cannot ask aright or expect to receive.

Let us know clearly what we desire, and desire that particular thing or condition more than anything else, at that moment; and as we ask or desire, let us remember that we are to believe that we receive. This latter is most important, since the mere mechanical action of the mentality or conscious mind—the so called "holding the thought"—is of small consequence in impressing the inner mind if it is merely a matter of lip-service, as is many times the case.

A little perseverance in the matter of asking in accord with the Universal Law will soon educate us to listen to intuition, or the inspiration of the Almighty, which quickly wires the word to the conscious mind, that we have received and we are satisfied to await the visible arrival of the desired good, of the coming of which we feel assured.

Next in importance to the impressing of the desire upon the inner consciousness is the matter of our having perfect faith in the process: first, in the law, that it is willing and able to do its part; and second, in our ability to meet the requirements of this law with ease and confidence. And if we faithfully and honestly do our part of the work, we may be sure of results, for it is only lack of faith that makes failure possible.

In speaking of faith, I mean the attitude of believing similar to that of a child—accepting the promises of Christ, as the child accepts the promises of its earthly parents—confidently expecting to receive the gifts offered, when we have rightly made known our desires to the great inner source of supply.

This childlike faith takes us directly into the limitless—the very soul of things; the storehouse of the inner realm, or the "substance of things hoped for"; out of which is created for us any and every thing and condition of which we form real mental patterns in accord with His law.

The matter of receiving or realizing depends upon us, and there is no greater truth than that "According to thy faith be it unto thee." Active faith opens the universal treasure house to us; while doubts and fears operate precisely in the opposite manner—dispelling and driving from us the things faith and confidence attract.

Having asked, believing that we do receive, let us not forget to each time give thanks that our asking or affirming has been heard and answered, and that the thing or condition for which we asked is ours. That is the promise, and these promises do not default. We are always the defaulters, when there is failure.

Combining the childlike asking and the gracious receiving is a wonderful help in impressing the inner realm with our honesty of purpose. The visible expression of the thing desired will soon follow, if we are alert to recognize the "signs of the times" and to welcome our own under whatever guise it makes its appearance. For the things coming to us from Infinity do not always arrive by the route we have suggested to ourselves.

And this brings to mind the matter of placing limitations as to how the desired good shall come to us. It is best to leave all avenues open rather than to point out what seems, to the conscious mind, the only way in which the thing sought can be expected to arrive. The ways of Universal Consciousness are wonderful and past finding out; and while we might be getting ready to welcome our good from the source we specify, it might knock at our door from another source and receive no recognition from us, so steadfast would be our attention upon the limited way chosen by the conscious mind.

The conscious mind should be encouraged to work confidently and expectantly, but always serenely and in a precise and orderly manner, without a particle of doubt or fear as to the accomplishment of the desired purpose; for said James, "He that wavers (doubts) is like a wave of the sea—driven and tossed. Let not that one expect anything of the Lord"—the Universal Law. Doubts and fears are impressed on the inner realm in the same manner as are believing and trusting thoughts; and with a mixture of both kinds we shall accomplish little that will be of value to us.

All Power is Given Unto You

Chapter 3

All Power is Given Unto You

All Power is Given Unto You

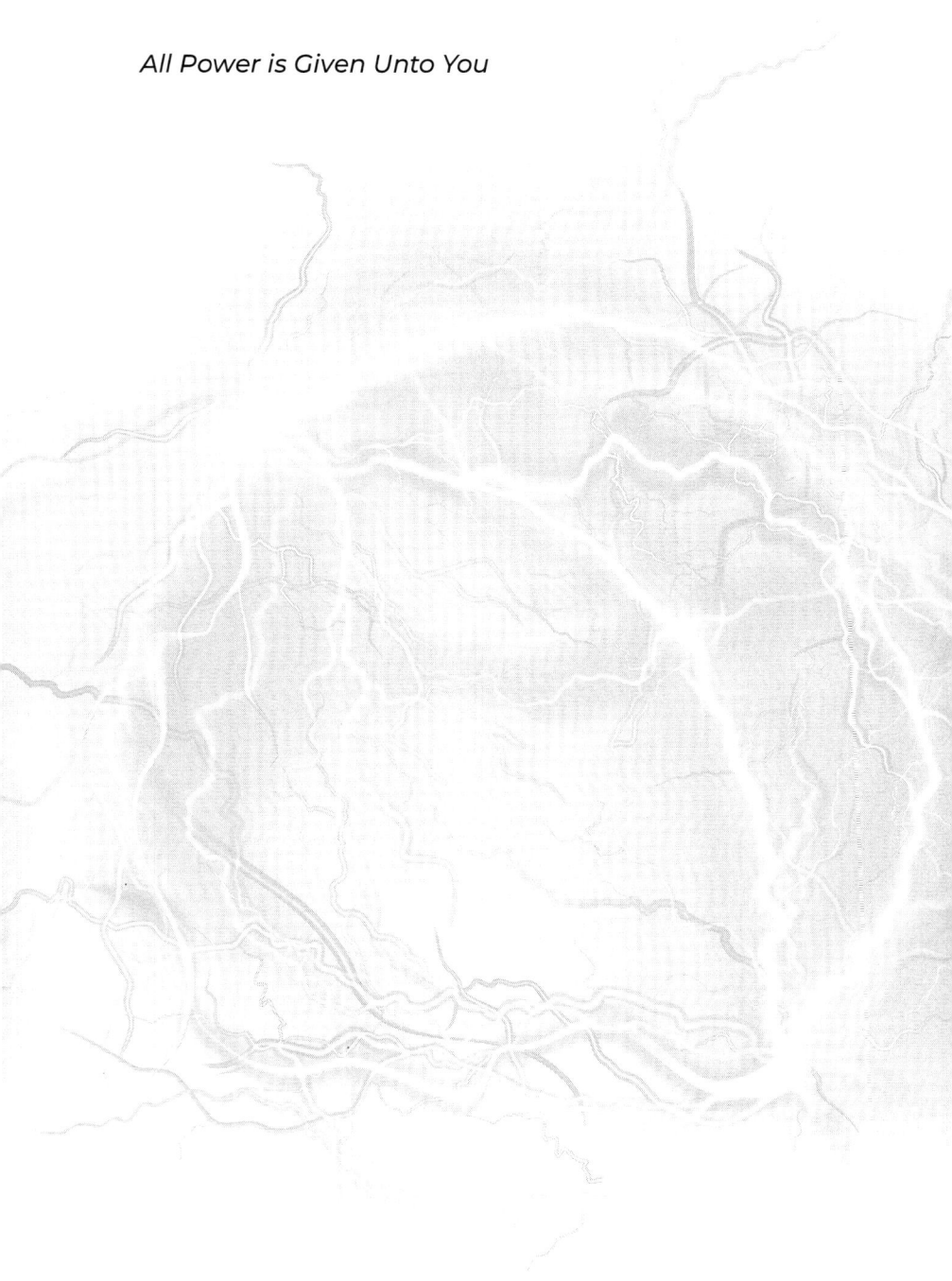

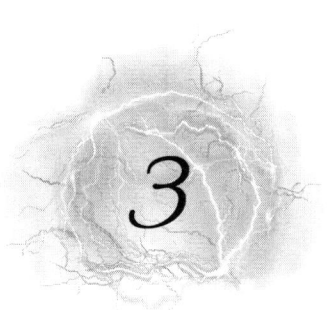

3

WITHIN each one of us is unlimited power, sufficient for our every need, if we will learn to carefully put it to work, with the determination of mastering every detail of daily living rather than allowing trifling things to enslave us. A little time daily devoted to the cultivation of the mental realm soon puts us in possession of a wonderful harvest, for the inner mind is indeed a "present help in every time of need," when we appreciate it and know how to accept its benefits.

The common custom of running hither and yon for advice and assistance as to the solution of our problems soon falls away when we discover that all we can ask or ever need in the way of help is within ourselves, ready to manifest or come forth instantly if we but seek it with "all our heart." Failure becomes impossible and with perfect assurance we may knock at the door of wisdom and knowledge again and again, expecting the desired results to follow as night follows day. It matters little who or what is against us if God, the All Good, is consciously with us. Then doubts and fears have no place whatever in our calculations.

To live a life of freedom and satisfaction, we must know what we are about. We must have confidence in our mode of procedure all the time and all the way. Experimenting with God's laws to see if they will work will not be sufficient, since that mode of living brings hope and courage today only to be followed with fear and discouragement tomorrow and really gets us nowhere; for while we may think ourselves quite filled with faith and courage at night, the morning may find us in exactly the reverse condition of mind, diligently at work destroying all we have previously built.

This, because we do not know the truth. When we do know it, and live that knowledge, we are through experimenting and confidently begin in the morning with renewed faith and courage, a little ahead of where we left off the previous night. And this means advancement along all our lines of endeavor, and desired goals are constantly coming into sight.

Mental processes are not unlike the physical, only because with our physical eyes we do not see the mind working, perhaps we feel it may not be a wholly reliable mode of accomplishment. But if we are willing to accept as authority the promises of our Father and go about our daily affairs of living, tranquilly and expectantly, we shall soon prove for ourselves that the real things of life are those which are invisible to the physical eye. We shall find ourselves going back to Paul's philosophy and re-stating his "The things which are seen are temporal but the things which are not seen are eternal."

The action of the inner mind is not unlike that of the phonograph. Under certain conditions, it accepts and records all that passes before it, and under certain other conditions it reproduces, with wonderful accuracy, all it has recorded. Not only this, but it will reach out into the realm of all knowledge, of which it is both an inlet and an outlet, and will discover for us the answers to our puzzling questions, solving for us our most difficult problems if we will, with real faith in its skill and ability to accomplish all things, apply to it for such knowledge as we need.

That the inner mind can do anything is true, but true only in this sense: It can supply the power, understanding, wisdom and ability to do the thing desired; but it is our part to consciously apply and make use of the material the inner mind brings into expression, before the desired purpose will be reached or served and the thing or condition desired attracted from the invisible—the creative substance all about us—into visibility.

Things and conditions desired rarely appear to us "ready-made" from the mental workshop. From it we obtain the "substance of things hoped for—the evidence of things not seen," but which we know exist for us (if we are in communication with the inner source of all knowledge), and will come into visibility when our faith is sufficiently strong and high to act as a magnet to attract these things into our lives.

In other words, we get from the inner mind the material from which we shape the garment, and we may fashion it as we will, from the least even to the greatest. Nothing is too good to be true, if we really trust the Universal Law and mark our course daily in accord with its teaching.

But we cannot think and talk of illness, nerves, lack, misfortune, disharmony of any or every kind, and expect the subconscious to take up and express for us as health, peace, power and plenty. Let us be careful and earnest in preparing the pictures we throw upon the mental screen, remembering that "As we sow, so also shall we reap," or as we think, so will the inner consciousness create and express in our lives.

If we look back a few thousand years, we shall discover that it was because of wrong thinking that Job recorded upon the inner mind the things and conditions he did not want. But as he thought, so it was unto him, according to his "The things that I have feared have come upon me."

And so the things that we have feared (perhaps without really being conscious that we feared them) have come upon us, and will continue so to do. For fear makes its impress on the subconscious mind, just as naturally as does trust; and everything that is impressed upon the inner realm will in due season be expressed. Our own—the things we create for ourselves—whether by faith in good or ill—is bound to come to us.

Thus to fear illness, lack, failure, harm or any undesirable condition, is to plant the negative seed in our mental garden, which will take root and produce a harvest after its kind, for men do not "gather grapes of thorns, or figs of thistles." Seed time and harvest proceed by the same natural law, whether in the mental or material realm.

The prize of health, happiness and prosperity—a life of satisfaction in every department—is worth striving for, since it offers physical, mental and material freedom. And it is ours for the choosing—so why sit down and long for it, rather than to rise up and accept and attract it into sight?

If desired results are slow in appearing, it is only because we have not plainly impressed upon the inner realm the thing or condition we seek. Our thought has been mixed. We have been trying to create or attract to ourselves too many different things at one time, and have dissipated our thought force and so lost the reality of our mental picture. We must learn to be positive in these important matters before we have a right to "expect anything of the law."

Faith is the power that makes all achievement possible, for when our faith is rightly and firmly placed in the subconscious mind, it becomes creative, and we then create for ourselves whatsoever things and conditions we desire. There is no guesswork or uncertainty about it. We may rest satisfied, knowing that our desired good is at hand.

This knowledge comes to us as inspiration from the Almighty, and we care very little about details. We know. We have arrived at the turn in the road where His guide-post says, "Having done all, stand"; and with complete confidence we await the outcome of all events of our lives, realizing that the inner mind is the open road to our heart's desire, and that there is no good reason why any of us should be "poor and in prison."

Chapter 4

The Secret of Success

All Power is Given Unto You

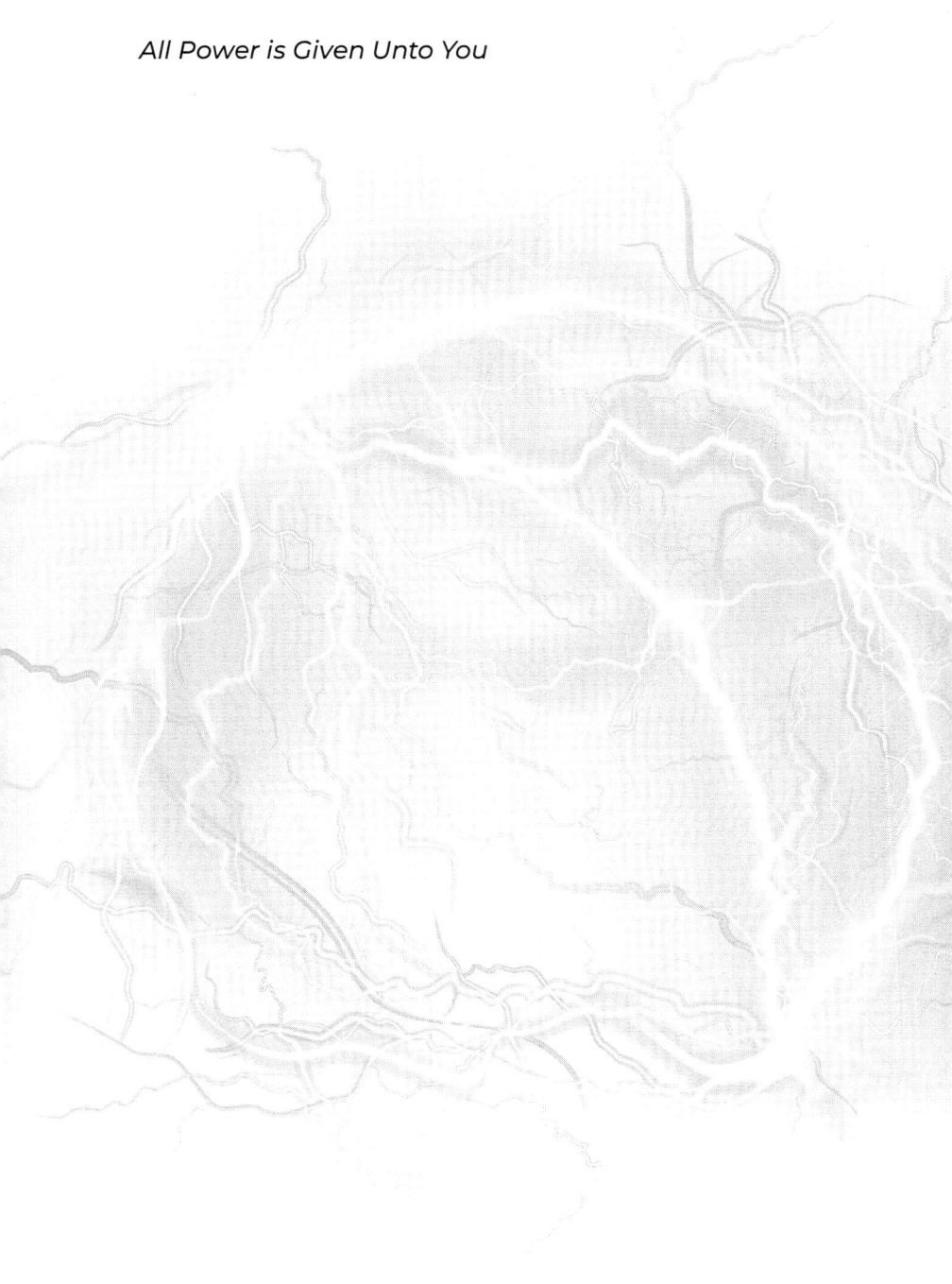

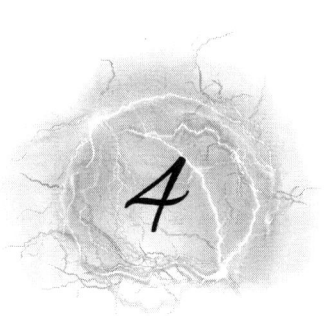

CONCENTRATION is the secret of success. Lack of concentration is the cause, of which a gigantic waste of human effort is the effect.

Steam, gas and electricity, when not concentrated or condensed, are not only practically valueless, but are tremendously destructive and harmful agencies.

The same is likely to be true of human intellect and effort. Mental power, rightly directed, can do anything that is desirable.

It is the same powerful agency when wrongly directed; and we are constantly seeing, hearing or reading of the destruction and trouble caused by this misdirection, or lack of understanding, of the mental processes.

Where waste prevails, be it of human energy, mental power, or any working or workable force or commodity, the harvest is likely to be poverty, illness, disharmony and failure, as a direct consequence or result.

The Creator and Controller of the universe has amply supplied our every need, and has given to each the ability to possess and enjoy our inheritance of "exceeding, abundantly more than you can ask or even think," if we are sufficiently interested to accept this legacy upon His terms,.

And what are the terms? "Ye shall know the truth and the truth shall make you free."

Each of us can quickly picture for him- or herself what it means to be free physically, mentally and financially. For until we are free in every department of life, we are not free.

An important portion of the truth is, "There is nothing either great or small, but thinking makes it so."

Do we know how to think? By this I do not mean do we know what things to think are right or otherwise. But, do we know how to really use the mental process effectively? Do we know how to fix or center the mind on a desired object and hold it there?

If the answer is "Yes," then we know how to concentrate; and if we know how to concentrate the mind upon the thing or condition we desire to manifest, we are in possession of the key to the kingdom of All Good.

But in every community we find quite an army of the "lame, halt and blind." Those who are not in possession of the key to the kingdom of All Good. Why do they not accept their inheritance and enter into peace, power and plenty?

For the same reason that we so frequently fall by the way ourselves. Lack of dependence upon the mental power as a reality. And perhaps the lack is so great that they have little knowledge of how to use this power to advantage, and so are unable to accomplish anything by its use.

Not infrequently have people said to me, "If people are poor, sick and unfortunate, all the thinking in the world can't make them otherwise, of course." And there is such an element of finality in the close-up of this decision that it is not an easy matter to persuade these people to try a change of opinion, and start on a new trend of thought.

If this change is made, however, and steadfastly

pursued in the right direction, a harvest after its kind is sure to be the result.

We have proven very many times the mistaken idea in the above argument, and do not hesitate to say positively that "If people are poor, sick and unfortunate," a small part of the thinking in the world can make them otherwise: and will make them otherwise, if that thinking is properly placed and sustained.

Do we desire better evidence of what is ours for the claiming than this: "And if ye ask anything, in My name, I will do it"?

What has thinking to do with that promise, do you ask? Suppose we try Paul's recipe for changing "people who are poor, sick and unfortunate" into those who enjoy health, happiness and prosperity.

How does Paul say this may be done? "If there be any virtue, and if there be any praise, think on these things"; and then going on in his attempt to plant the right seed thoughts in the minds of the Philippians, the thoughts that should create for them the same conditions that we desire to enjoy, he said: "For I have learned in whatsoever state I am, therewith to be content." And again, that none should fall into an ambitionless state of faith without works, he adds, "I can do anything through Christ which strengthens me."

That is truth, but not any more truth for Paul than for us; and if we will learn to concentrate on the things and conditions we desire, rather than to fall into the habit of thinking that "all the thinking in the world" cannot make people who are "poor, sick and unfortunate," otherwise, we can establish in our lives whatsoever things and conditions we desire.

Let us drop argument to the contrary, and try the effect of thinking on the conditions we desire, regardless of what conditions appear to have taken possession of us.

To those who will do this intelligently and honestly, will come many pleasant surprises. By this process chronic invalids, even though of years' standing, will be healed and made every whit whole. Conditions of poverty and its attendant ills and inconveniences will soon begin to blossom into ease and prosperity; while fear, doubt, worry and discouragement—the almost universal cause of which illness, unhappiness and poverty are the effects—will fade away, to return no more forever.

Concentrated thought is all-powerful. But, it is powerful for good or ill; so that we must be careful of the mental processes, if we desire lives of satisfaction.

The business of learning to harness the mental realm, and so control and conserve its power, is worthy of our most careful and intelligent consideration. And it is not the difficult matter many people appear to believe it to be. A little daily practice will soon enable us to use the mental power for the accomplishment of any and every right purpose; rather than to seem to be used by it, or to allow it to rust and become almost unusable.

Concentration upon whatsoever subject we desire may easily be made a mental tool for the accomplishment of our purpose, if we will, like Paul, believe in the truth that we "can do all things through Christ which strengtheneth" us.

The well-trained mind works almost automatically, with very little conscious effort, if it is only supplied with worthwhile material upon which to operate. If, however, one chooses to think on conditions of illness, lack, fear or negative thoughts of any kind, the harvest is sure to be of like nature. "Like attracts like" on every plane of existence, be it mental or physical, and "As we sow," whether in the earth or the mind, "so also shall we reap." This is one of Nature's laws, and works with precision.

We can teach ourselves to think uninterruptedly upon whatsoever we will, and to hold the mind firmly to the subject upon which we choose to think, if we care enough about it to determine to be steadfast in following orders, minus all argument of what we could do if we were otherwise situated, or if others in the household or neighborhood were in sympathy with our endeavors.

Teachers and lessons upon concentration can help us only insofar as we accept and immediately put into practice their teachings. A passive knowledge of truth may be better than no knowledge at all; but until we prove for ourselves the accuracy of each theory advanced, we have little conception of its real value.

It is when we, mentally, throw our whole weight upon the solution of a problem that things begin to clear up all about us. We do not then try to think about this thing in which we are tremendously interested. On the other hand, it is difficult to keep the mind off it. Thinking about it is our business, and a delightful business, too, and we dislike to banish it, even temporarily, from the mental workshop while we attend to the commonplaces of the day.

That is concentration of the kind that wins. Easy, too, isn't it?

We may, however, possess all the knowledge possible as to how to harness and drive the mental dynamo, but until we take the reins of government in our own hands and start the machinery upon the specific task we desire to perform, our knowledge will avail us very little in the way of results.

Knowing how to concentrate the mental power is one thing. Concentrating this power for the purpose of arriving at the solution of our problem is quite another.

Not that the knowing how is of no avail. But all knowledge is merely theoretical to the individual until he or she makes use of it by practice; by putting to work, if you please, all that the theory presents.

It is in the mental realm that we create for ourselves our own.

Concentrated thought upon a specific thing or condition will create for us that thing or condition; and from some natural source it will be attracted to us, or will attract us to it.

This is quite as true of seeming ill as of what we call good.

The mental process is precisely the same which creates the things we fear, or about which we fret and worry.

It is the mental power that does the work, following the pattern we hold before the mind.

This is why we harm ourselves so greatly by thinking and talking of illness, trouble and disharmony of any kind, thus keeping them constantly before the mental camera, to become photographed on the creative substance all about us.

It is from this creative, or God, substance that we create the things and conditions which come to us—be they good or ill—by mentally relating or connecting ourselves with them.

It is our privilege to "Choose ye this day whom ye will serve." But universal law has ordained that having chosen we must stand by our choice. So that it behooves each of us to learn to choose wisely and well, or to sow such seed as will produce for us the harvest we desire. We may become masters or slaves. But in either case, we must pay the price.

The book of Job tells us that "There is a spirit in man and the inspiration of the Almighty giveth him understanding." This is God's way of talking to us, His children, daily; but until we know how to properly manage the mental machinery, or to center the intuitional faculty, much of this inspirational knowledge will be lost to us since we shall not know how to listen to the messages.

If we fail to listen for our answers when conversing over the telephone, we know what happens. We lose the information we seek.

When seeking information and help from the spirit within, we need to practice listening, or concentrating the mind on the information sought, in much the same earnest and expectant manner. By so doing we shall be able to arrive at a solution of even our most difficult problems.

The Universal Consciousness is no respecter of persons, and meets its obligations with each individual in precisely the same manner when we ask aright. That is, when we have earned the right to receive the thing desired.

Man was created in the image and likeness of God, and He has no favorites. To each of us He says, "Ask what ye will, believing in Me, and it shall be done." Nothing in the Gospel indicates that one individual has any preference over another.

It is true that some seem more closely in touch with the Universal Power for accomplishment than others. But this is wholly due to a difference in the degree of enlightenment, occasioned by study and concentrated meditation upon the truth.

An accomplished pianist or violinist gives years of diligent study to the chosen work. That one of us who had given little or no time to thinking of and practicing music would hardly attempt or expect to shine as a musician. He might have quite the same power, ability, wisdom and intelligence as the accomplished musician, and yet not have cultivated these qualities to any degree whatever so far as music is concerned.

The same is true of spiritual understanding. All of us are one with Infinite Spirit. Infinite Spirit lives within us, and yet some of us hardly accept this as truth, and so realize practically nothing of the wonderful power that is within us and is the real part of us.

When we determine to give to the development of this inner power the time and concentrated thought, or study, that it would be necessary to give to any other important matter in which we desired greatly to excel, we shall not only discover the truth, but we shall also discover that the truth applies in all its beauty and force to us individually and to every detail of our living. The desires of our hearts will be attracted to us, not because of luck or chance, but because we know how to reach out to the supply of All Good that is all about us, and by our honest, concentrated effort, select for ourselves our own; and bring the same into manifestation or visibility, with the same ease and naturalness that the Great First Cause said, "Let there be light, and it was so."

The individual differences to be observed in persons we meet are largely a matter of concentration, or knowing how to use the mind efficiently. What is commonly called a "liberal education" is frequently of small account to the one possessing it; the reason being that he or she has been taught something of a good many things, but is unable to master any portion of this knowledge for actual use. The knowledge is there, but in a confused mass, as it were, and the possessor is utterly unable to profit by it.

Just as the music is in the piano or violin, but absolutely useless, until concentrated study has taught us to harness the tones to a nicety in accord with the law of harmony.

Concentrated thought power will solve your problem, regardless of how great a puzzle it seems today. Learn to concentrate the mind on the thing or condition you desire to understand, for a sufficient length of time daily, and soon you can say, as did Paul, "I can do all things"; and all essence of boasting of your ability will have vanished.

What has been done can always be done again, and each time ought to be done with greater celerity. But if we tell the world we can't do a certain thing, it will believe us; taking us upon the estimate we place upon ourselves and our ability.

Not that the world will think the thing cannot be done, because we declare that we cannot do it. It will likely know it can be done, and with small effort, on the part of a positive thinker.

Negative thinking hardly accomplishes much, until a change of thought comes about; for just as "He can who thinks he can," so is it true that he can't who thinks thusly.

That we can do anything by thought is a simple and wonderful truth.

Concentrated thought connects us with the inspiration of the Almighty, and enables us to obtain the solution of our problem.

Right here I want to say that concentration is not the intricate or impossible matter many people appear to consider it. I refer to this, because so frequently students tell me they have found it impossible to "concentrate" or to "enter the silence."

Either one means nothing more difficult than getting quiet and thinking "on these things," as Paul says. Choosing the subject for thought, and meditating in the quiet, as we wait for inspiration to quicken or enlighten our understanding in relation to the matter about which we need additional information or enlightenment.

We might just as easily, and with great profit to ourselves and the world, form the habit of concentration as to form any other habit. It is only a matter of doing our own thinking upon the things in which we are interested, rather than to allow others to make our decisions for us.

All Power is Given Unto You

Chapter 5

How to Concentrate

All Power is Given Unto You

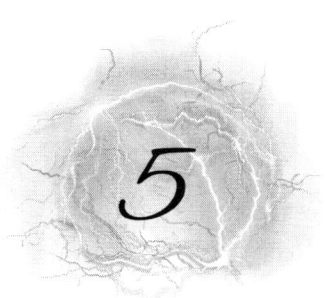

H ENRY WARD BEECHER tells how he learned to manage his mind, at a time when this ability was really the turning point in his life; and so great was his satisfaction when he realized that he knew how to cast out his mental anchor, and hold fast to the line of thought he desired, that he declared himself willing to part with all his earthly goods before parting with this mental treasure which opened to him the door to the kingdom of all knowledge and power.

It was in slavery days, and the influential men in his church were averse to freeing the slaves, while Mr. Beecher was for freedom. Attempting to stand for what he believed right caused misunderstanding in the church, in fact seemed likely to close it, leaving him minus his salary, and he had no money at the time with which to support his family.

The situation became very grave and he worried about it constantly, going back and forth, mentally, over what might happen, but making no progress for himself or the church.

Suddenly he determined to think the matter out once and for all, and following his habit opened his Bible for the purpose of directing his mind in the beginning. He looked down upon the words, "Let your conversation be without covetousness." Inspiration helped him to understand that that referred to his little salary, and that he was not to borrow further trouble as to where his living was coming from.

Then he read, "Be content with such things as you have." He said, "I haven't many things, but I'll be content with what I have," and that was settled.

He looked again, and the next was ample reason why he should be content. "For," it said, "I will never leave nor forsake thee. So, that we may boldly say the Lord is my helper and I will not fear what men shall do unto me."

Many times before he had read this, but never with any live application to himself and his needs. Now the white light of the mind within him shone upon it.

He laid down the Bible and said, "All right, Mr. Elders, shut up the church if you have a mind to. I'm not afraid to speak the truth before any man that lives, since I have this message direct from my God."

And he concludes, "Perhaps a thousand times, since that day, has this experience come back to me, when a difficult problem has come up for solution. But it placed my feet on the solid rock of faith in God, and taught me to apply His truth to my problems, intelligently. It taught me to use my mental power for the purpose for which it was given me."

Fear, doubt and worry dissipate and waste this power, making it of small account in our lives; while it offers to us satisfaction and freedom if we know how to accept its bounty.

Positive thinking reaches out into the great sea of all knowledge and grasps the truth for which we are ready, and which gives peace and confidence to the heart and mind, in the understanding that with God, the All Good, "all things are possible."

Concentrated right thinking recognizes this as truth. And when we learn to consciously connect with All Power, which is in us and all about us, and keep this line constantly open, all things are likewise possible unto us.

When we do not quite see how we are to go on with the task in hand, let us do as did Mr. Beecher—think from whence cometh our strength of purpose, on any and every occasion. This will give to us the keynote, which will enable us to work out the whole symphony.

To go back to the Psalmist's way of accomplishment: "My help cometh from the Lord (the Law) Who made heaven and earth. He will not suffer my foot to be moved," will prove wonderfully satisfying to us if we have the courage and patience to prove our faith in this process.

With this truth as a reason for the faith that is in us, if we will concentrate our mental power upon the thing we desire to manifest, the result will be "exceeding, abundantly more than we can ask or even think."

Let us try standing still, mentally, while we see the salvation of the Lord. To those who think it necessary to call upon Tom, Dick and Harry, with the hope of hastening or influencing the working of the Law, it will be enlightening to learn how much trusting God and fearing nothing will achieve.

The power of concentrated thought is the greatest power in the world, and until we decide to acquire the habit of individual thinking, we shall be only about one-third efficient in making use of the opportunities that come to us daily.

Paul's advice that regardless of all appearances we think on the Good is even better than it may appear at first reading; since when we begin to really think on the Good, we cease to think on the other side of the equation; and soon the apparent other side takes unto itself wings and flies away and we discover that there is only Good as a reality in life. That all seeming otherwise, is merely the absence of the real. An appearance, as it were, which is overcome and cast out when the light of wisdom is allowed to shine upon it from the within.

To have a time and place daily for the study of, and meditation upon, the use and meaning of life will prove of great value to each one of us. We not only need to know the Universal Law, but we need to think how we can apply every portion of this Law in our methods of living.

Few of us would start on a short journey without first learning all we could about the details of the trip: the shortest and easiest roads, most convenient and comfortable hotels, as well as places of interest it would be possible to visit.

But the journey through life is frequently pursued from day to day in a sort of hit-or-miss fashion.

Most of us know that there is a law of living, even though we do not call it the universal law, but we give little time to informing ourselves as to its requirements, or to ascertaining how closely we are living in accord with its mandates. Nor do we realize that we have a perfect right to our inheritance under it, when we have proven our title to that inheritance by directing our daily living as it tells us to do.

Strong and broad are the promises of our Father: "Ask what ye will, believing in Me, and it shall be done." And as though determined to convince us of His willingness to enrich us, He says, "And if ye ask anything in My name, I will do it." Yet these promises seem to mean practically nothing to the great majority of people.

Some claim that they have "tried this asking and it didn't work" with them. That they asked precisely as the Law prescribes, although they didn't much think they would get the thing asked for; and they didn't. Consequently, they have decided that God either thought it best that they should not have the thing desired, or that the promises refer to spiritual things only.

Either conclusion, if found to be the correct reason why the thing desired was not received, would wholly invalidate the above as well as all of Christ's promises.

But what is wrong with much of our asking?

James tells us that if we ask and receive not, it is

because we ask amiss. And that does not quite answer the question, save in raising another:

What is asking amiss? Which I would answer by saying that asking amiss is asking for something we have not been graciously willing to earn the right to receive.

When we are seeking aid through the agency of Christ's promises, there can be but one reason for failure in receiving. That recited by Christ to His disciples when they, having failed in a case where He easily succeeded, asked why they could not do the things that He did: "And Jesus said unto them, Because of your unbelief: for verily I say unto you, If ye have faith as a grain of mustard seed, ye shall say unto this mountain (your particular problem), Remove hence to yonder place; and it shall remove; and nothing shall be impossible unto you."

Honest and active faith, unmixed with fears and doubts, never fails to create for us and bring into visibility the thing or condition for which we have expectantly asked; together with the "exceeding, abundantly more than we can ask or even think"— the latter coming to us in accord with His "good measure, pressed down and running over."

The grain of mustard seed, tiny though it is, gives no thought of worry to its supply or growth, any more than does the giant oak.

Rather, it confidently reaches out its tiny arms or branches into the creative substance all about it, and draws to itself everything it needs for life and growth.

It does not give its time and power to scheming and planning as to how it can grow to best advantage next week, next month or next year. It gives no growing energy to plans for rainy days or sunshiny ones. But, it accepts from the great Universal Father Mother all and whatsoever it is ready to use, now, this moment, in its growth, and attends strictly to its business of growing .in its own natural way, giving no heed whatever to tne fact that the giant oak is taller, hardier, or able to attract more attention to itself. The purpose of the mustard seed is to become a natural and healthy mustard plant; not an oak tree.

When we have a like simple faith in our position and plan of life, our asking for whatsoever we desire will be sufficient to bring into manifestation the good for which we are ready.

Many of us will solve a problem, upon which we have been busy for some time, if we will do some real thinking upon the mustard seed's manner of growth and fulfillment. It will tell us why much of our asking has been apparently unanswered.

The mustard seed knows it's simple need, and, reaching out into the Father's storehouse, claims and accepts its own; no more and no less. But all the time keeps happy and busy with its own affair of growing into the thing Nature made possible for it.

We have only to do likewise, and we may say to our mountain, "Remove hence to yonder place" and it shall remove, and nothing will be impossible unto us.

Knowledge awakens power. But knowledge only comes to us by concentrated mental work. Concentration, with hopeful expectation upon the problem we have determined to solve by the light of the inner wisdom.

Another of the rescripts handed down by that great teacher, Paul, is: "He that cometh to God must believe that He is, and that He is a rewarder of them that diligently seek Him." He also tells us that we must not only keep the letter of the Law, but the spirit of it as well.

If we are not manifesting or attracting into our lives the things we desire, let us see if we are keeping both the letter and the spirit of the law pronounced by the Creator; because James tells us that if we fail in "one point, ye may be held guilty of all."

Sometimes a very little in the way of correction of our daily habits will open the source of supply for us, in ways that seem quite marvelous.

It is impossible to bargain with Spirit, desiring to "give so much" and receive whatsoever we will.

Serving God means having one master and serving Him to the best of our ability, and with all the heart.

When we do this fully and freely, all things will be possible unto us.

Until we do, we have not proven the title to our inheritance, and the matter of demonstrating the things and conditions we desire will be more or less uncertain and unsatisfactory. Let us "think on these things."

If our asking has seemed to be in vain, this does not indicate that ours is an unusual case, calling for special treatment by the Universal Consciousness. We are all created in the image and likeness of God, and we carry with us insurance against accident of every name, kind and nature, if we so believe, and if we steadfastly trust this insuring power, which is all and in all, and which is the life within each one of us.

Each one of Father's great family is in line for the same treatment from Him; but all of us do not so believe. The reason being that we have not thought it a sufficiently important matter to warrant our careful and concentrated investigation. It takes time and our best mental effort to thoroughly understand God's perfect law of protection; but the understanding is worth all it costs. Few things pay such satisfying dividends.

Many of the new perceptions of truth do not accommodate themselves to the old racial ideas and beliefs, but that does not matter. It is the truth we want, if we would be free; and it matters little what our ancestors believed to be right and proper.

Let us have a time and place daily for meditating upon, inviting and receiving the inspiration of the Almighty, which is ready and waiting at all times to enlighten our understanding upon any and every subject upon which we need assistance, if we will only get still and listen for the message.

We need to examine the universal law for ourselves, with thought and care; accepting or rejecting each statement or promise, in accord with our willingness and determination to live the same.

To declare a statement faithful and true, or beautiful and inspiring, is of no account if we intend to live quite opposite to it. Faith without works is dead; and saying that we believe or love God's law and then straightway proving, by the things we do, quite the reverse of our words will profit us nothing when we are weighed in the balance, since He knows "even the thoughts of our hearts."

It is our privilege, and right, to be founded on the solid rock of faith in God, the All Good; if we care enough about it to do for ourselves some real thinking upon the subject.

Twenty minutes, daily, of concentrated thinking upon the truth uttered by our Father, "Be still, and know that I am God," would soon prove the open sesame to all knowledge for us; helping us to accomplish the things upon which we have set our hearts. Let us take time each day to get quiet and do some real thinking. We shall find it a wonderfully profitable and satisfying investment.

The old-time beliefs which made God (the All Good) appear like a stern autocrat, ruling with an iron hand and sending upon His children, when it was "His will," all kinds of trials, troubles and tribulations, which we were told we should "accept with resignation"—it being a deserved punishment—no longer ring true. They have been overcome with good.

The so-called New Thought encourages us to be happy, and to live the truth, as it is expounded to us by our elder Brother with Whom we are one. All knowledge within us assures that we can have the desires of our hearts, if we are willing to ascertain for ourselves how we may create and attract the same into visibility.

This is not a difficult matter. On the highest

authority we have this promise: "Ye shall know the truth, and the truth shall make you free." Does not that make it worth our while to discover what is truth, and so secure for ourselves freedom?

And freedom means that we are free in every department of our lives, physical, mental and material.

Concentration is the key to this treasure house.

It is not the part of Universal Consciousness to force us to accept our inheritance, and there is more for us to do than merely to cry, "Lord, Lord." We must determine to know what is the will of the Father, and to live that will as honestly and naturally as we are able. That means satisfaction.

It is because we so scatter and dissipate both our mental and physical force that we fail in attracting into our lives the things and conditions we desire. Concentration will bring all things to pass for us, if we will ask in faith, nothing doubting, and expect only the good to come to us because we have made "straight the way of the Lord," the Law.

This does not mean that we are to tell this great Consciousness how it can answer our asking. Its work in our behalf is done even "before we ask," and it is our faith in this, as well as in every other of Christ's promises that will act as a magnet to attract into sight the thing or condition desired, if we go happily forward with the task in hand, realizing that "He doeth all things well."

Let us keep in mind that teachers and leaders cannot live the truth for us. They can help to illuminate it, perhaps make it plainer and more easily understood for us. But after that, it is "up to us" individually to live it or otherwise, as we determine.

The title to our birthright is so clear and simple it is surprising we are so slow in proving it, and in taking advantage of our inheritance under it. It is also surprising to find that it is nothing other than the old racial ideas of limitation of various kinds, coupled with our own mental indolence, or lack of thinking upon the real business of life, that prevents our enjoyment of all the privileges of freedom, even to the "exceeding, abundantly more than we can ask or think."

Chapter 6

Creative Power of the Word

All Power is Given Unto You

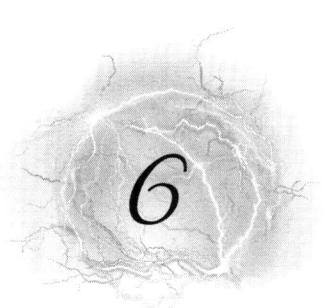

I N the first chapter of Genesis we may read: "In the beginning, God created the heaven and the earth."

"And God said, Let there be light and there was light."

"And God said, Let there be a firmament, and it was so."

"And God said, Let the waters under the heaven be gathered together unto one place, and let the dry land appear: And it was so."

"And God said, Let us make man in our image, after our likeness, and it was so."

A few thousand years later, Christ, who was likewise God, said, "He that believeth on me, the works that I do shall he do also; and greater works than these shall he do." All of which, when understood and believed, would seem to present a simple and accurate working hypothesis for the business of creation, as practical and workable today as in the olden time, if our faith is equal to the task of breaking away from the old racial beliefs and habits, and taking God, with Whom all things are possible, at His word.

In each of the instances above quoted, creation was quickly and naturally accomplished upon the speaking of the word by the First Great Cause, called God. This really illustrates how accurate and simple is the work of creation, when the word is spoken with power into the creative substance which fills all space.

"Let us make man in our image, after our likeness, and let him have dominion over everything"; and as simply and generously as that there comes to each one of us, as our inheritance from our Father, not only the power by which we may create by the word, but all the wonderful attributes of this First Great Cause which make us all-powerful if we accept our inheritance of all and every good thing and condition for which we can ask or of which we can even think.

Truth it is that we, being made in the image and

likeness of our Creator, have within us the power to speak into being "all things, whatsoever we desire," if we will employ the same effort and care in learning to use that power that we exercise in obtaining education and experience of far less importance and value.

Of course the important starting point in this work is to believe that we do possess this ability to speak into being the specific thing or condition upon which we fix the mind; and until we do really believe it we can hardly expect much in the way of results.

Believing, or faith in the word of the Master, is the peg upon which hangs the whole system of asking and receiving, under His law or word. It is the "capstone of the corner," in all things relating to spirit, and its ability and willingness to do for us all that Christ has promised to "those who believe."

Daily, we are creating things and conditions in our lives, by the power of the spoken word; and whether desirable or otherwise, we have each created for ourselves and attracted to us the conditions in which we find ourselves.

If these conditions are satisfactory, it is due to the fact that we have thought and talked of right things. If they are not satisfactory, it is not the fault of the First Great Cause. He has not ordained that we live in one condition or another, other than to create us in "His image and likeness," and give to us dominion over all things, under certain terms, which are plainly made possible for us in His will.

If we have failed in observing the terms of that will, and so have been unable to obtain our legacy under it, it is not Father's fault; it is our own, and it is never too late to correct that fault, if we honestly and earnestly determine so to do.

We must prove our title to the inheritance coming from Spirit, just as we must do when receiving a legacy under any human will; nor is this a cause for displeasure or criticism of His gracious intent. It is only an opportunity to prove our faith in the universal law as it stands upon the statute book of the ages, as the law of right and satisfactory living; and until we so regard this law, we shall not please God.

When we have lived the whole law, and have not failed in one point, as James states it, we may, with perfect faith in the All Supply, begin at once to speak into being, and so cause to appear in our lives the things and conditions we desire, and for which we have an immediate use in our plan for large and selfless living.

The All Supply, or creative substance all about us, holds all and everything we desire, now, and is more willing to give to us of its abundance than is the most affectionate earthly parent to give good gifts to a well-beloved child.

"Ask what ye will, believing in Me, and I will do it" is the strong and significant promise each one of us may claim when we have honestly fulfilled our part of the contract, of which this promise is a part.

What is our part? "Believing in Me"; and until we believe we have not earned the right to receive, by making this promise a law unto ourselves.

The matter of applying the truth to the solution of life's problems is so grandly simple most of us persist in overlooking it. We are not unlike the little fellow who made his first visit to the country in quest of Mayflowers, and returned home at night bitterly disappointed because he had been able to find none, although he declared he had diligently climbed to the very tops of the highest trees in the forest in search of the flowers.

And so we likewise make too hard work of applying to the universal storehouse for the thing or condition we desire. In the commercial world it is a simple matter for the different departments of a business to obtain such supplies as are needed. Perhaps a blank requisition must be properly filed with the supply clerk, and the articles required are delivered.

The matter of receiving our promised "exceeding,

abundantly more than you can ask or even think" is really not more difficult than the above, when we have properly filled out our requisition and forwarded it to Spirit's storehouse. And by this I mean when we know and comply with the universal rules which plainly tell us how our supply may be obtained. This is precisely the same as the employee in the commercial house must do. Every rule of the house must be regarded and obeyed, if one desires quick and unquestioned service.

And so before we greatly profit by the ever-present helper we must understand what is expected of us, and be ready to run quickly on Spirit's errands. We must know what is the universal law, before we can intelligently determine to obey it; but when we have possessed ourselves of this knowledge—and it is not difficult so to do—the rest is easy.

In manner similar to that chosen by the First Great Cause to bring the world into manifestation, may we bring into manifestation in our world (our bodies or material affairs) such conditions as we desire, if we will first prepare ourselves to make the decree with confidence; having obtained for ourselves the right to expect that decree to be established unto us.

The matter of individual creation is a fact, and as we think and speak into the creative substance all about us, so shall we create for ourselves good, if we so determine; or ill, by precisely the same process, if we allow the mind to dwell upon undesirable things and conditions.

Good is ours the instant we make the decree, if we will so believe.

Let us remember, too, that it is not our business to establish the decree; that is the part of Universal Consciousness, or God.

But having decreed or affirmed that health is ours—or spoken the word of health for ourselves, let us accept health as a reality, and be done forever talking about disease and disharmony of every kind.

Let our historians write of us, "They said 'Let there be health in my body and affairs.' And it was so."

Having uttered a decree, we may confidently await its establishment—knowing the thing or condition decreed is ours, and will materialize as soon as we remove all barriers and "make straight the way of the Lord"—the Law. "See, then, how that by works a man is justified, and not by faith only. Faith without works is dead."

Our works are the proof of our faith, and so long as we have faith in a task we will diligently work toward its completion. And so it is not sufficient to merely think we would like a certain thing, and decide that we will expect it to appear. That would be faith without works. But having thought or mentally patterned the thing, we may go on and speak into being, and so cause to appear the thing desired.

If we are failing to demonstrate or manifest the things and conditions we desire, there is probably but the one reason—that uttered by Christ, two thousand years ago—"Because of your unbelief." Saying we believe in good as the only presence and the only power profits us little, if we are soon after found speaking into being conditions we do not desire, and which indicate our lack of freedom and satisfaction.

Are we "troubled and worried over many things" in the material world? We do not need to be. The same agreement with universal law that will create health and cause it to become visible will likewise create, and materialize for us, as supply, if we will steadfastly speak the word of abundance and cease for all time thinking and talking of poverty, lack, economy and like negative and unreal appearances.

There is no limit to our material inheritance, save as we utter the decree of lack; and thus by our spoken word separate ourselves, seemingly, from the Source of All Good, which is our supply, and can never be exhausted, or in the least degree reduced in its giving ability.

"Let there be plenty in my life, with which to do the work of Him who sent Me, in the broadest way possible," if intelligently spoken into the creative substance all about us, with perfect faith in the truth, and with the realization of our oneness with it, will supply us with any and every thing we are ready to use today, for large and selfless living.

Health, happiness, prosperity, peace, power and plenty—anything and everything, even "abundantly more" than we are able to mentally compass, will come by the same route—that of speaking into being, and expecting to receive the thing or condition decreed.

This means, however, that we must do the things, after having spoken the creative word that will prove to our fellows that we have faith in this process of creation; for the poet reminds us of a simple statement of truth in her declaration:

> "Nothing can keep thee from thine own
> But thine own doubtful mind.
> To one who knocks, each door unlocks;
> And he who seeks, shall find."

All Power is Given Unto You

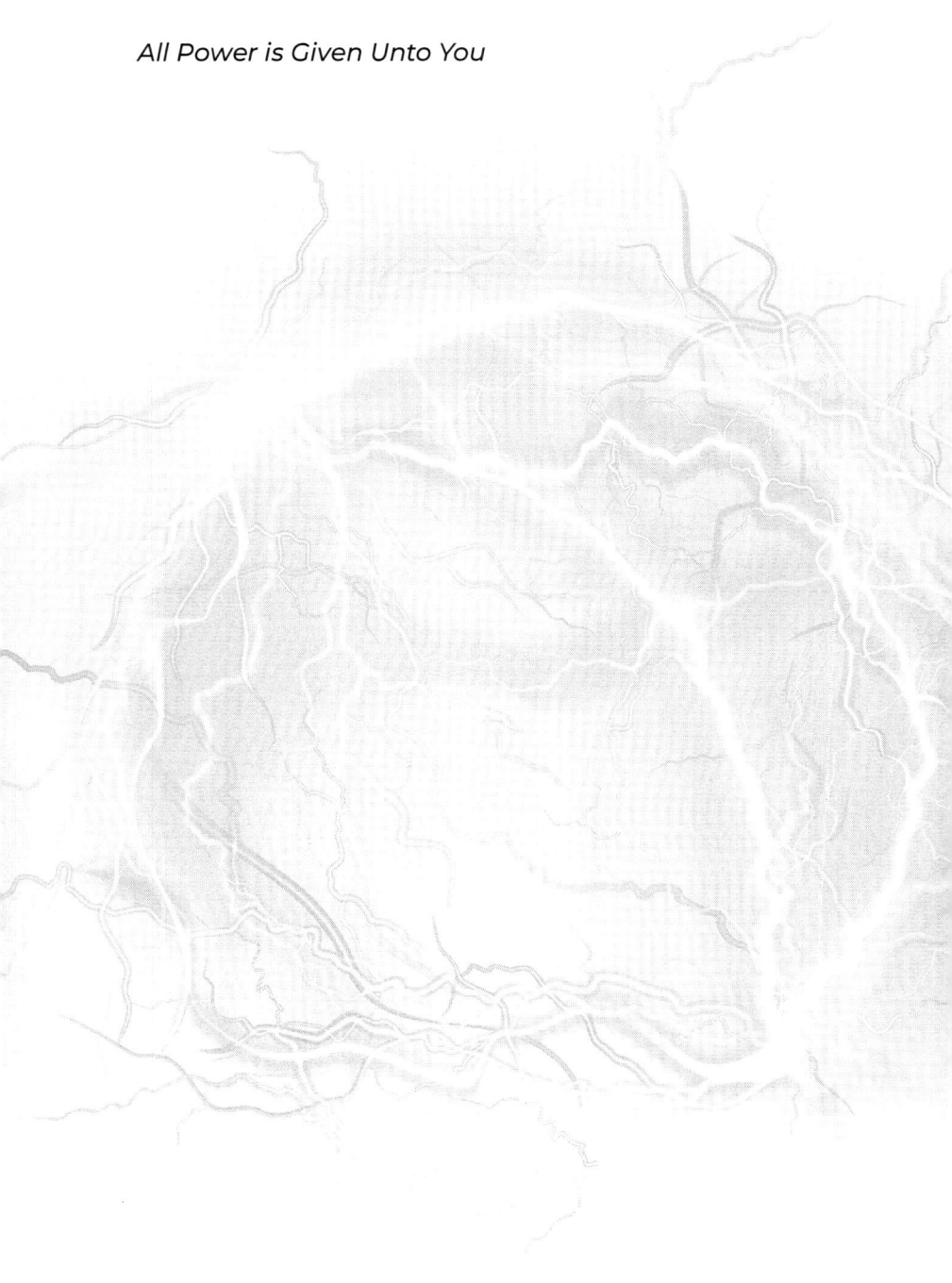

Chapter 7

How to Use the Creative Power

All Power is Given Unto You

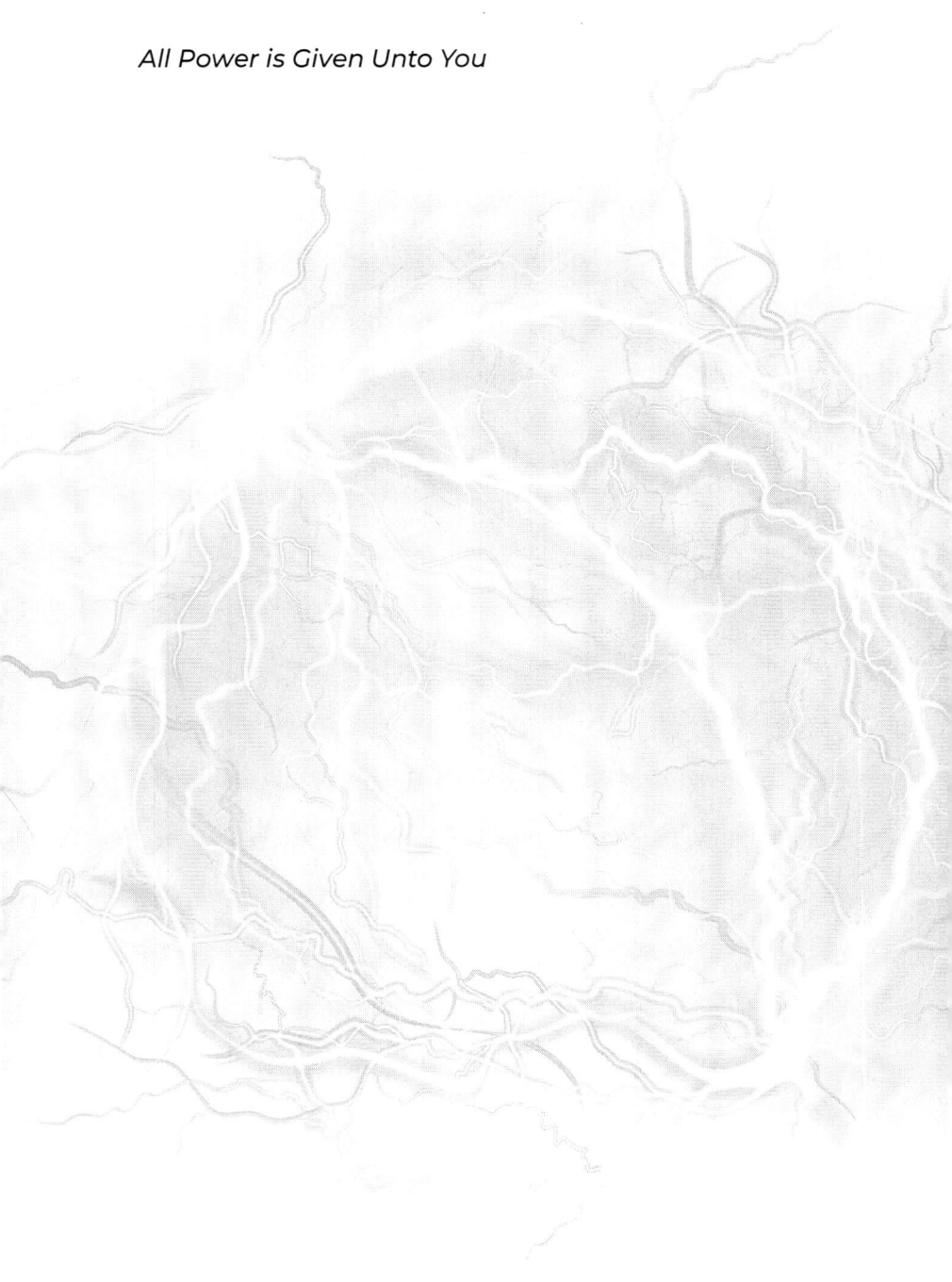

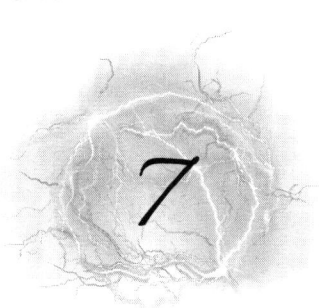

THE power to create for ourselves only good—only such things and conditions as we desire, is within us; and the ability to reach this realization is a matter which is in our own hands. It is our privilege to make of our lives what we will: To stand for something, or to be inventoried of small account because of mental indolence.

Again, it is well to conserve our creative energy, using it only in the creation of desired conditions; and to keep the conscious mind wholly free and unhampered by doubts and fears, which merely dissipate and waste the thought force, and the physical energy as well; producing for us nothing of value, if not deliberately hindering us in the accomplishment of our most cherished plans for worthwhile work.

This is where a tremendous leakage of mental power is too often allowed to take place. Most of us know more or less of the theory of creation by the power of the word. Perhaps we believe it possible to create for ourselves the things we desire, by the power of the spoken word; and yet, while in possession of this knowledge, which may not be clearly established in the mind, we go on daily speaking into being in our lives, things and conditions we by no means desire, and which can bring to us not the slightest satisfaction.

Why do we continue to so enslave ourselves? Why feed the inner mind with anticipated trouble, and so connect ourselves with negative thinkers everywhere, when we know that every thought must create after its kind and that "Birds of a feather flock together" in the thought realm, just as naturally as in any other department of life?

What shall it profit us if we sit up straight and declare "I am fearless" for twenty minutes, and then spend the next several hours discussing, and even enlarging upon, the things of which we say we are afraid? Afraid to go out, lest we take cold; afraid to eat certain things, lest they will not agree with us (they don't need to agree with us; it's our privilege to do the agreeing); afraid to drink coffee, lest a headache is the result. A good, Christian lady told me recently she "adored cheese" but "it did not like her," and she was afraid of some very harmless-looking little sandwiches that were offered her. And so we go on and on, until the clock reminds us it is time to sit straight in our chair again for twenty minutes and affirm, "I am fearless."

Perhaps this sounds somewhat unreasonable and overdrawn, but let me tell you that it is not, and it is the real reason why many people, who call themselves disciples of the so-called New Thought, and who, it may be, have been trying to practice some of its teachings for years, have made little or no progress in the matter of overcoming fear.

It is no less an affirmation when we admit, even in our thought, that we fear to do thus and so, than though we set aside a special time and place for so thinking and speaking into visibility these fears of undesirable conditions. It is not the time or place that creates; it is the spoken word which must create after its pattern.

That we set aside a time and place for thinking "on these things," as Paul said, and communing with the Spirit both within and without (for it is omnipresent), is largely for the purpose of establishing system in our mental workshop, as well as proving our faith in Spirit's ability and willingness to do all it has promised to do for us. It knows when we are in earnest in our work of communion, when we feel the necessity of serving it over and above all things else, and when the uttering of these affirmations, for a certain length of time, is merely an experimental matter with us. Lip service, so far as Spirit is concerned; performed, it may be, because someone has told us of rather unusual results obtained by so doing. Thus we might utterly fail to get the spirit of the work, or the realization of from whence cometh our aid.

Every real and honest teacher doubtless feels the truth of the "Of myself, I can do nothing. It is the Father within me that doeth the works." Until the student realizes that truth, and feels the necessity of keeping carefully his or her appointments with Spirit, over and above any ordinary matter which might arise, the seeming miracles of healing, physically, mentally or materially, elude his or her grasp; and results are likely to be unsatisfactory, where instantaneous healing, or changing of conditions, might easily be possible and obtainable if faith in the process was sufficient.

Faith in the power of the word, let us remember, is the very capstone of the corner, in the matter of creation. And "Without faith, ye are nothing," and little or nothing can be obtained. Merely "entering the silence" or "holding the thought," so-called, is along the line mentioned by Paul as "faith without works"; and until we realize that the silence is everywhere, and always, and that instead of "holding the thought" twenty minutes a day, we must hold it twenty-four hours a day, we have not really made a fair and promising start along the King's highway.

When we arise in the morning and say, "I am absolutely free and unafraid," and then proceed to live that absolute freedom and unafraidness all during the day, and take it along with us when we retire, not many things will bother us; for the world makes way for that one who knows where he is going, and despite all things else faces fearlessly forward. Even the old fashioned, much-talked-of-devil takes care to keep from underfoot, and fades away, rather than take chances of being side-tracked or stepped on.

We need not stop to reckon with the matter of "taking cold," if we are properly careful as to dress; and "whether we eat, or whether we drink," if we "do all to the glory of God"—All Good, no harm will come to us, for "He will not suffer my foot to be moved."

When we really recognize and trust the Great Consciousness and Power which spoke this universe into being, there is nothing in all the world to fear; and we go about living the freedom this knowledge awakes in our hearts; which knowledge creates, and attracts into our lives constantly, all things, whatsoever we can ask or even think, as fast as we are ready to receive our inheritance, of "every good and perfect gift."

To a much greater extent than most of us realize, our thoughts are the architects of our fortunes, for it is in the mental realm that we first formulate our decrees; from thence, speaking the creative word into the substance all about us, which is to create for us the condition or thing that will do its part in making or marring, to a greater or lesser degree, a portion of our lives.

A life of satisfaction must be built in accord with a working hypothesis in which we have confidence. Before we shall demonstrate or manifest our desires with precision, we must know exactly what we want to accomplish. When we know how to present to the inner mind a pattern that is correct as to detail, then will our efforts become constructive and of real value, both to ourselves and to our fellows everywhere with whom we come in contact.

A few minutes set aside daily for meditation, known as "going into the silence," may be better than nothing in this line; probably is, since it indicates a certain kind of dissatisfaction with present conditions, and a desire for betterment. But let us remember that a few minutes used constructively, followed by some hours given to destructive thinking and speaking, can hardly produce for us anything worthwhile. We must first take time to diligently sow the seed, before we can confidently expect to reap a satisfying harvest.

When we really care enough about obtaining a specific thing or condition to determine to know the law by which that thing or condition can be obtained, and to steadfastly live that knowledge, we shall surely achieve our purpose, for then it is that our faith and works agree. Our creative words are fostered by our acts, which follow. We believe that we have received and this positive state of the outer mind is impressed upon the within and soon begins to bear fruit, by expressing in our lives more than we have asked or even thought, in accord with our Father's promise.

Active faith soon attracts into sight, from the substance all about us, the thing for which we are ready; and as often as otherwise, Father uses one of His children as the direct messenger of His good tidings. But the message comes no less from Almighty God, because of being delivered in His perfectly natural way. Perhaps I can best illustrate this truth by a little experience which has just come about, and is a direct answer to a call for aid made upon Universal Consciousness.

A publisher, for whom I have done quite a little manuscript work, recently asked me to quickly review Emerson's *Essays* and the *White Cross Library* by Prentice Mulford, choosing from both such ideas as appealed to me as truth, and with these truth ideas in mind, to prepare a simplified statement of how the mental realm can always be depended upon to present a solution of every problem with ease and precision, if unhampered by doubts and fears.

Without knowing just where I could find a set of the *White Cross Library*, I agreed to prepare the manuscript, feeling that the spirit within would be equal to any emergency which might arise. But faith without works is dead, as pointed out by Paul, and so I immediately began sending out calls for the needed books, by writing to various publishers, asking them to see if they could get the set for me.

Soon I decided this was not the way to procure them, since results were most unpromising. The local public library did not have them, and I discussed with Universal Consciousness the idea of getting someone to borrow them from some distant public library, if no better way opened; thanked It that I was sure of obtaining them, and left it with Father, while I went about my next errand.

Some two days later I unexpectedly met on the street a lady who had done us a good turn, and stopped to say a word of thanks. She began to tell me that she was going soon abroad, and was getting things in condition to leave, and would like to send to my home, to be kept until she called for them, a set of Mulford's *White Cross*

Library; and she had never heard me mention a desire for the books. No, she knew nothing of my direct need, but she was the chosen link of Divine Mind to connect me with it. Universal Consciousness chose to work through its beloved child in this way, in supplying the need of another of its children.

It is no less a direct result of Divine Help because coming through one of God's children. He more often works in this natural way than in a supernatural manner. But He always hears and answers, if we will poise ourselves and expect the thing or condition we are ready to use, to be quite as ready to be used of us.

Active or living faith in the Universal Consciousness—a realizing knowledge that we are at one with it, assures us that our decrees are "established unto us," and we prefer that the world shall "know us by our fruit," rather than to judge by much speaking as to what we could do if our environments could only be made to our measure. We have spoken into being our present environments and conditions. If they are not satisfying, we need not go on creating and re-creating like things and conditions; but we may at any moment select a new pattern by which we may completely change undesirable things and conditions into, or for, the most perfect conditions which we are able steadfastly to hold before the inner mind and speak into being.

All Power is Given Unto You

Chapter 8

How to Speak the Creative Word

All Power is Given Unto You

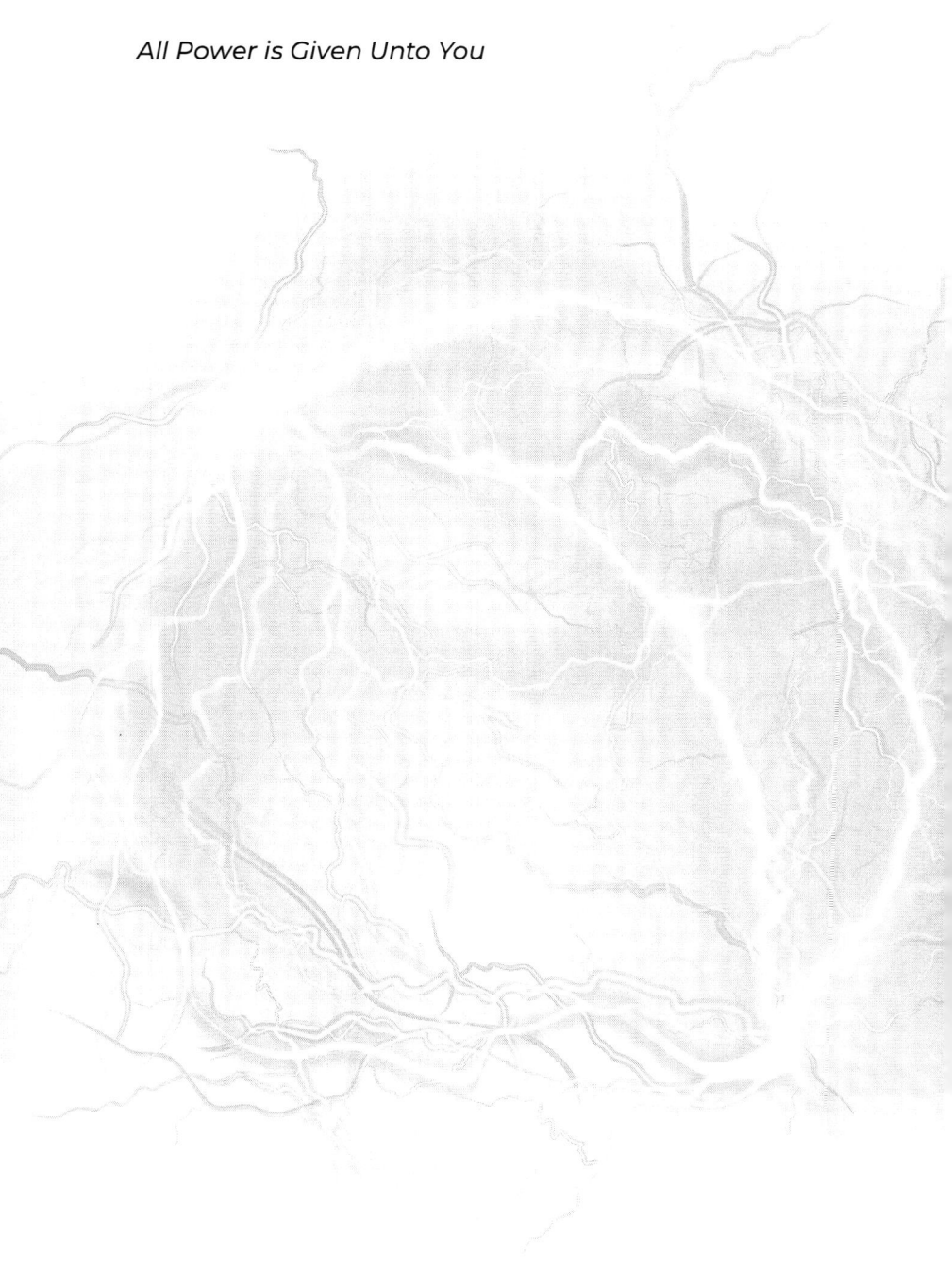

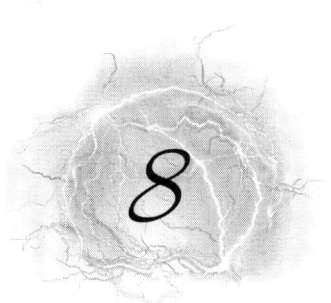

IN what seems excellent authority, we are told that the original use of language was not wholly that of conveying thought; telling what was going on in neighboring households; who had stylish raiment and the estimated cost thereof; or discussing the details of our "operation," or other varieties of so-called disease. But that the real purpose of the privilege of speech being given to man was that he, made in the image and likeness of his Creator, might be able to exercise a like power in the use of the word for the business of creation. That he might be able to speak into being, and attract into visibility, all things whatsoever he should rightly desire.

But like most of the other wonderful gifts of

God to man, he has tried to elaborate upon their original plan for use. He has not been satisfied to create rightly, by the use of the word; but he has used it quite as frequently, and is using it, to create wrongly. Just as he has taken the rules of health, and of his dominion over all things, and attempted to amplify or more agreeably fit them to his idea of man's need.

Had we followed the law as pronounced by the great Creative Word, when speaking the world into being as to our food, it is doubtful if a great variety of the diseases—appendicitis, encephalitis, arterio-sclerosis, phlebepatitis, phlegmhymenitis, and quite a large bookful of others, about as easy to spell and pronounce as the above (I practiced on this spelling for some twenty years, as a reporter), could ever have found a repository in the unsuspecting mind of one of God's children.

Of our food question He made short, plain and wholesome work in His "Behold, I have given you every herb bearing seed, which is upon the face of all the earth, and every tree, in the which is the fruit of a tree yielding seed: To you it shall be for meat."

Plain enough, even though we had no direct commandment saying, "Thou shalt not kill"; and yet at the tremendous risk of being afflicted with such a ridiculous sounding disease as phlebepatitis, or its brother in disgrace, phlegmhymenitis, we shall continue to find those in our midst who will object to a daily menu in accord with the idea of the Great Source of All Good, which had in mind loving kindness to every living thing upon the face of the earth.

Again, had we accepted our dominion "over the fish of the sea, and over the fowl of the air, and over the cattle, and over all the earth, and over every creeping thing that creepeth upon the earth," as Father evidently intended we should do, namely, by exercising that dominion precisely as we desire All Power to exercise its dominion over us, what might not this attitude toward the life under us have brought to us? "As ye sow, so also shall ye reap," and "As ye mete, it shall be measured to you again."

The fish, the fowl, the cattle; (God bless them every one); but in their language, as they talk with Universal Spirit, and It knows the thoughts of their heart language, as It knows ours, what can they say of our dominion over them? To be sure we have sanctioned, if not ordered, that some of them be murdered, that we might eat of their flesh and be merry, apparently quite overlooking what the Great First Cause said was to be to us for meat.

May not this suggest, if not explain, why so frequently we find ourselves "poor and in prison" to some of these diseases? Let us think these things well over, and if there are seeming causes of dissatisfaction in our lives, we may be sure they are occasioned by our having "missed the mark." And then it is our privilege to ascertain just how we have failed, and to devote ourselves untiringly to curing the cause of our trouble. God, the All Good, does not visit calamity upon us; but we, by wrong thinking and doing, attract it into our lives.

If we look back over the record, we shall note that Christ did all His wonderful works, that of healing the sick, raising the dead, stilling the storm, feeding the multitudes, as well as manifesting many other unusual and remarkable proofs of omnipotence, by His word, which seems to indicate the correctness of the statement that the original business or intent of language was that by it man might become his own creator.

It seems a pity that we have accepted the habit of wasting so much of this valuable accomplishment in "riotous living," so to speak. Or in thinking and talking about things and conditions we really do not desire, but which we continue daily to speak about; thus creating appearances of poverty, lack and dissatisfaction, when by the same process we might just as readily, and much more profitably, create such things and conditions as we desire.

Let us decide to be done with destructive thinking and talking and to begin today to conserve that wonderfully profitable asset, the spoken word, for the beneficent and gracious purpose for which it was given to us.

On every side are we surrounded by the creative substance of Universal Consciousness, ready and waiting to be fashioned into "whatsoever ye desire," if we have sufficient faith in this Consciousness to provide, and steadfastly stay by, our pattern. But we may, by using a wrong pattern, mentally, dissipate and waste very much of our creative power; that is, we may by fear and worry thoughts create and attract into our lives the very opposite of the thing we desire; but which undesired things will be created by the same thought and word power (our general conversation) as would the things and conditions desired.

Christ has warned us of the importance of the use of language, in His "But I say unto you, that every idle word that men shall speak, they shall give account thereof in the Day of Judgment."

"For by thy words thou shalt be justified (established in the Good, if we speak forth Good), and by thy words thou shalt be condemned" (to the unhappy and distasteful conditions in which we, by the use of the word, place ourselves mentally).

Let us, then, determine to disregard any and all appearances that are not quite as we desire; and speak the word of Good on any and every occasion, thus proving our faith in the promises by taking God, the Great All Cause, at His word.

Said Christ, "When ye pray, believe that ye receive,

and ye shall have." Let us take that promise at its face value and when we have made known our needs, by the word, expect the desired things to in due season, become visible as they will do in perfect accord with our faith.

To think and talk of ill, lack, misfortune—any negative or undesirable condition, as likely to visit us, is really to challenge, or deny, His power and love to do for us all that He has agreed to do. And such thoughts dispel and destroy, just as naturally and by the same law, as positive or constructive thoughts build, and attract into sight.

A matter of supreme importance is the care and management of the mental kingdom or realm; so much so, that we will find it profitable to drop many of the so-called daily duties or pleasures (which in the real business of life are practically worthless), while we devote much time to thinking upon the law or principle by which all things were and are created—the Universal Law that governs all life, even that degree of life we call the spider or the fly, and "every creeping thing that creepeth upon the earth."

Yes, we can have the things and conditions we desire; but in order to do so, at all times the words of our mouth and the meditations of our heart must be acceptable in His sight; and we shall find it profitable to add this petition to our daily communion with Universal Consciousness; and then if we will see to it that our thoughts and words do not cause us to stray from the straight and narrow path, we shall soon realize that we are constantly moving forward toward the land of promise we long to possess.

Faith in God (the All Good) will prove for us the open sesame to any and every thing and condition we desire; but until we have this faith, and know we have it, the promises of the great First Cause are as worthless to us as are the promissory notes of a man who is bankrupt. Not because these promises are in the least of uncertain value, but because we have failed to prove our title to our inheritance, under them, even though our failure may appear to be only in the "one point," which James tells us, may "hold us guilty of all."

In proving our faith in God, or Good, let us remember that works mean more in the eye of the world than words; and this will likely continue to be so until we learn to more nearly appreciate the value of words; and until we determine to at all times use our words constructively, and with care, rather than to pour them forth in the thoughtless and aimless profusion which will not only help to destroy us, and dissipate our ambition, but may also have much to do with causing dissatisfaction and unhappiness in the lives of many of our associates.

It is both interesting and satisfying to read the story of Christ's ministry upon the earth and note the simplicity of His sayings; but the greater interest comes, as we realize how, by the power of His spoken word, He instantly healed the sick, raised the dead, and did many other so-called miracles. And it is really these latter works that lend the practical and helpful interpretation to His sayings.

Wherever He went, it was much the same. The seeming miracles he so easily accomplished by speaking the word, established His fame and really convinced even the people who slandered and dishonored Him that His teaching was far more than a beautiful theory regarding the purpose of life.

And then as He is getting ready to depart—His work on this plane being finished—He leaves us this inspiring message: "Verily, verily, I say unto you, he that believeth on Me, the works that I do, shall he do also; and greater works than these, shall he do; because I go unto My Father."

This is a portion of the "good measure, pressed down, shaken together and running over," He offers to all who will believe in Him and His truth.

Most of us, very likely, have read His truth again and again. Perhaps we have thought it beautiful, maybe inspiring, and yet we have not really understood it and have made small attempt to apply it in our daily business of living. Instead, we allow the mental workshop to become a "house divided against itself," and to constantly produce results over which we are unhappy.

Again, some of us are anxious to prove to the little community in which we live that we have a part in a variety of interests and activities. And with this intent, we divide our mental house into so many parts that little that is of account is accomplished in any line.

It is the "eye single" that eventually has the long list of accomplishments to its credit. And it is this singleness of purpose that in a comparatively short time will take us a long way toward reaching the longed-for goal of satisfaction.

The Universal Law works with precision, bringing to each of us the things and conditions with which we connect ourselves, mentally, be they either good or ill. If we are clogging life's machinery by attempting to force it to run in our way, rather than to gladly and joyfully run with it, in God's way, we shall surely be the losers. And we shall continue to be losers or failures until we determine to get in line with truth, and live the life of freedom which is the birthright of each one of us.

All Power is Given Unto You

Chapter 9

Your Mind Dynamo

All Power is Given Unto You

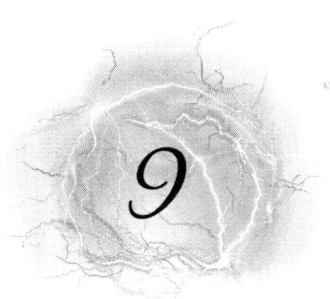

"**A**S a man thinketh in his heart, so is he." No greater truth is on record than this, which was uttered by King Solomon, some few thousand years before we heard much of the so called New Thought.

But evidently Solomon had found out that the greatest power in the world was the inner consciousness.

Since Solomon made the above discovery, much has taken place in the world. Many wonderful things in the way of time and labor-saving devices have been discovered, but nothing yet has dimmed the strength of the statement at the beginning of this page. Nor has anything modified it in the least. As a cure-all for any and every condition needing cure, we still offer it with perfect confidence in its efficacy, precisely as Solomon pronounced it all those centuries ago.

The mind is the All Power at work within each of us; and because of this, "all things are possible unto us."

When we recognize this truth, and put out of our lives all the things and conditions that disagree with it, confidently expecting the success which comes of truth's accomplishments, we do the things that are possible unto us. We become the all-powerful children of God, the All Good.

Any of life's problems that come to us individually may be solved by the right use of the mental power, if we combine with the mental work the action it suggests. The mental realm is the workshop, in which we may work out for ourselves whatsoever we desire, from the least even to the greatest of life's problems and events.

Wisdom, knowledge and power within each of us is limitless if we will learn to search for it intelligently.

"There is a spirit in man, and the inspiration of the Almighty giveth him understanding," is something more than a beautiful theory or proverb. It is a declaration of truth, and when we believe it with sufficient faith to daily take time to "enter into our closets" and listen for the sermon that the great inner consciousness will gladly preach to us, we shall be able to come out into the world and do things. Things, perhaps, that today seem to us well nigh impossible, because of our lack of understanding, or confidence, in this power within ourselves. But it is truth that, by its application to the problems we need to solve, we can solve them, regardless of how difficult they may now appear to us to be.

Life is by no means a matter of impossibilities. With God all things are possible, and when we really learn that we are one with Him, that we, His children, are ourselves Gods, if you please, we know that the God power within us is all-powerful.

Then it becomes a matter of devoting a little time daily to getting acquainted with this inner power—the God within us; and as fast as we grasp or understand the simplicity of the plan of the great Universal Consciousness, we seem to blossom into the truth that we can do anything we need to do.

If we would grow in wisdom and understanding, we must take time to be still and know that these treasures are even now within us.

They are there just the same, even though we

make no use of them. It is as though we had in the closet the key to all knowledge, but not knowing exactly how to use it, we decide to get along with such knowledge as we have at hand, sparse though it may be. Unhappy and dissatisfied, perhaps, and wishing we could make a better intellectual showing, but lacking the determination to acquire for ourselves such knowledge as would enable us so to do.

If, without much in the way of payment, we could find someone who would do the work for us, we would gladly have it done; but lack of faith in its worthwhileness prevents us from putting forth much effort to increase our mental equipment.

Likewise, a lack of faith in the healing power of the Gospel prevents many people from making much effort in the way of "searching the Scriptures"; and it is only by doing this that we acquire confidence in the promises therein contained; which confidence is the open road to physical, mental and financial freedom.

The matter of living effectively is wholly "up to us," individually. Life is a contract between each person living and that person's Creator; and neither can protect each side of the contract but each must do the part prescribed.

For example, Christ says in that greatest sermon on record, after having discussed several of the subjects that are a sort of bone of contention to many of us, and which cause a great deal of the world's trouble: "Therefore, I say unto you, Take no thought for your life, what ye shall eat, or what ye shall drink; nor yet for your body, what ye shall put on. Is not the life more than meat, and the body than raiment?"

And then He goes on discussing the birds, the flowers, and the subject of food; and tells us that our Father knows we have need of all these things.

"But," He says, "seek ye first the kingdom of God, and His righteousness; and all these things (the material things, about which we so greatly worry and doubt) shall be added unto you."

Our part in fulfilling this simple and gracious contract is first to know precisely what it is, what it says we are to do, and then to do to the letter what He prescribes.

What will be the outcome? When we have performed our part of this contract, we shall find that the part of the work to be performed by Universal Consciousness is done; and we shall begin to attract into visibility in our lives the things and conditions we have long, perhaps, been dreaming about and saying are "too good to be true."

"As a man thinketh in his heart, so is he." And the very day we think of the truth, as truth, and prove our faith by our works, we will begin to reap the rich and abundant harvest that is ours.

The Universal Law offers to each one of us satisfaction in all our ways; and that we remain unsatisfied is not the fault of the Law. That we do not know how to obtain this satisfaction is not an injustice of the great First Cause, but is rather a matter of indifference or choice on our part. Either we have not cared enough about obtaining our birthright to determine to know how it may be obtained, or we have chosen to spend our time and effort for other purposes than learning, first, what is the truth; and second, in living that truth at the cost of all things else.

The Law opens the door to us freely in its "I am the way, and the truth and the life," and we may study it at will. But, the Almighty does not force us to know the truth, or to live it, if we know it, in order that we may have the freedom that is ours at any time we have earned the right to have it.

Concentrated right thinking is the sure prophecy of its own fulfillment; and this ought to be sufficient incentive to decide all of us to get acquainted with the working power of the mental realm.

By the energized power of the mental workshop, health, harmony and prosperity are being established all over the world, wherever that energized power is rightly directed.

Let us remember that it is a creative force just as much, if wrongly directed; but creates after the mental pattern held in mind. A wrong pattern will give us the reverse of health, happiness and satisfaction, and will mean time and labor lost in retracing our steps; so that it is wise to at all times think on the harvest, as well as to know what are the rules of sowing the seed.

There is no disease—save as thinking makes it so. We are what we think we are, be it ill or well, good or so-called evil. The conditions called disease by the medical schools are really conditions of dis-ease, caused by breaking some law or laws of Nature—the great Universal Consciousness.

When we have righted the wrong, the dis-ease will become perfect ease.

Righting the wrong will have made us easy in mind first; and when the correction has become impressed upon the mind—the within—it will at once begin to express in ourselves and our surroundings.

That one who is ill today, in appearance, does not need to remain in that condition, if he or she will determine to change the thought current, and begin at once to hang health pictures on the wall of the great within.

It is never too late to turn about and retrace our

mental steps; and we will always find the latch string of Father's treasure house on the outside. Even at the eleventh hour He allows us to enter and partake of so much of the hospitality as we are able to accept and apply to our needs.

We must not, however, expect the Universal Mind to change its law, that we may thus be accommodated. It could not do this, if it would, without first rearranging the whole scheme of Nature; since it is not a matter of its listening to our petition, or our needs, and deciding that it will allow us to have the thing we desire—that it will send to us that thing—or that it will be better that we do not have the thing for which we ask.

That would invalidate many of its positive promises as to our receiving the thing for which we ask, and we know that He did not "come to destroy the Law: but to fulfill," both the law and the prophets, for He goes on to say that not one "jot or tittle shall pass from the law until all be fulfilled."

As fast as we meet these laws in every particular, and so prove our respect and love for them, our faith will attract into our lives all things whatsoever we ask or even think—if we have made ready to use these things intelligently and unselfishly.

Let us not make the mistake of believing it sufficient merely to think we would like certain things and conditions, because it would make living easier for us; and expecting these conditions and things to seek us out and thrust themselves upon us, because we "believe in New Thought."

The "Simon-pure" New Thought does not teach anything of the kind. It tells us we can have the things and conditions we desire, if we care enough about them to "go after them" legally—that is, by observing both in letter and in spirit the universal law, which makes us heirs to any and every thing and condition for which we have a real use.

To beg others to exercise this knowledge for us will likewise be insufficient. We must have within us so much of confidence and respect for the Supplying Law that we know that Law, and know we know it. This puts into our hands and hearts the key to peace, power and plenty; and takes out of our hands and hearts the key that would lock up, and keep for our own use, anything that should be passed on to our neighbor and which would make easy and comfortable his way.

All Power is Given Unto You

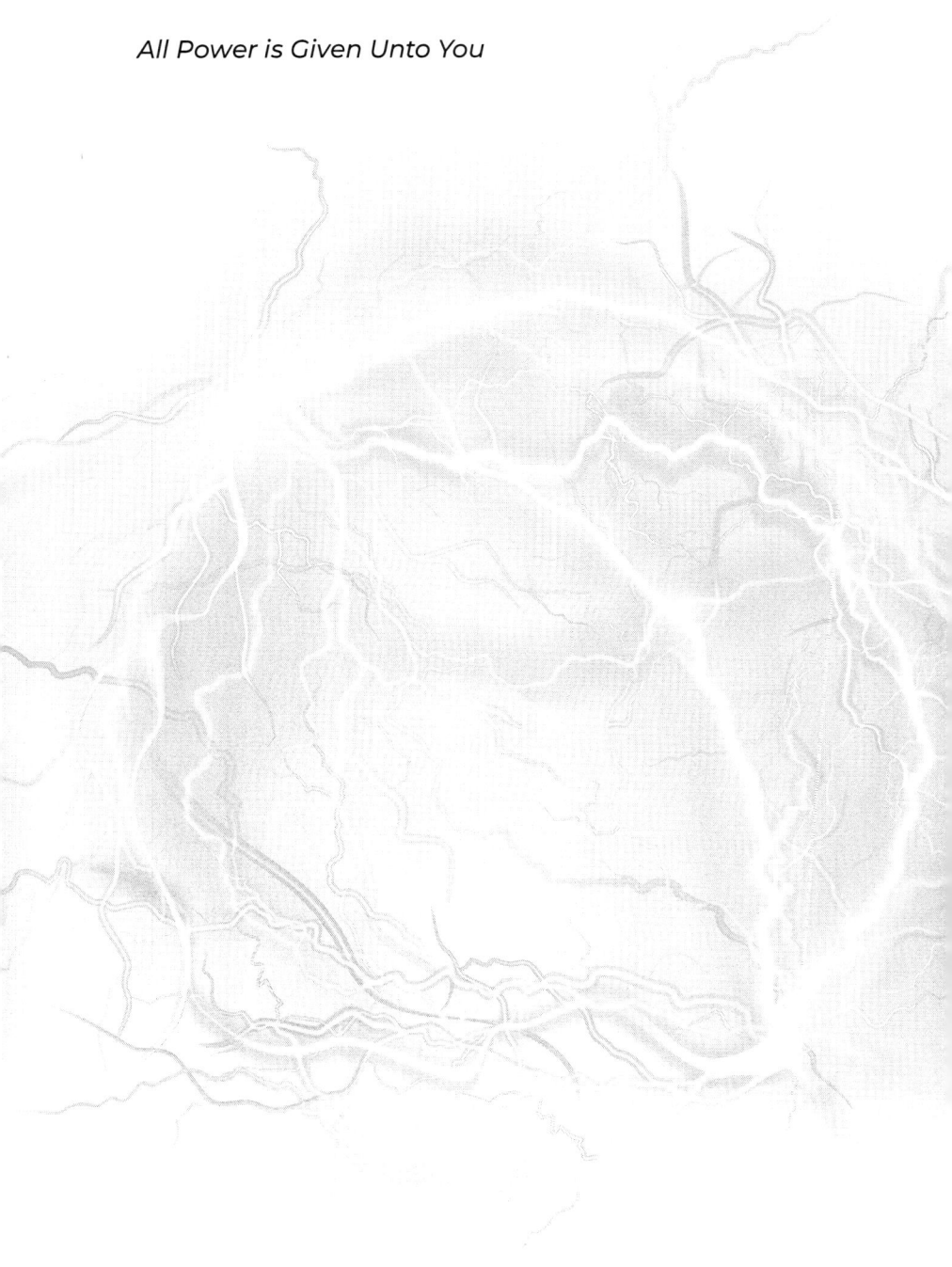

# Chapter 10

As Ye Sow

All Power is Given Unto You

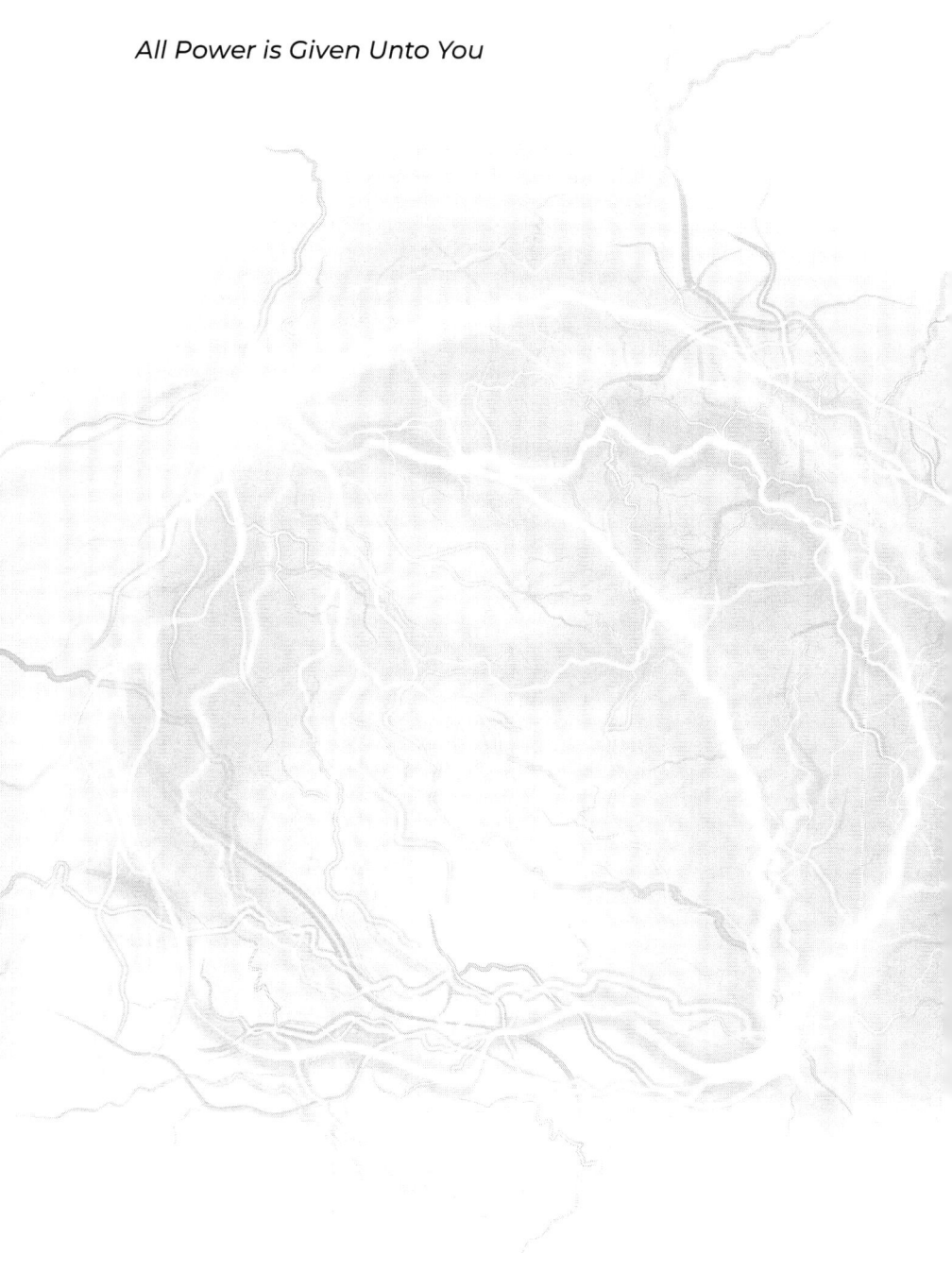

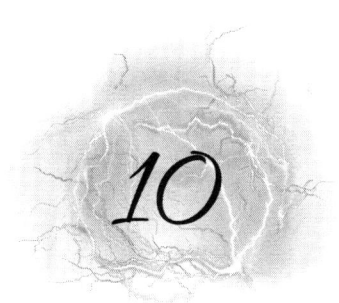

ONE of the greatest obstacles to demonstrating our desires is selfishness. We desire so much for ourselves, and give so little heed to the real needs, perhaps, of our neighbor. It is well to remember that a portion of His law is, "As ye give, so also shall ye receive," or "As ye sow, so also shall ye reap."

Many times we quite overlook this instruction, and go about begging the law to enrich, prosper and help us, in various and sundry ways, while we, apparently, quite disregard its injunction as to what we are to do, first, for it, and for ourselves.

Spirit holds no "red figure" sales; and if we are looking for bargains from it, we will first need to prove our worthiness of receiving the same. It requires us to, in a measure, prove our faith in it by being as willing and glad to give out of our good as we are to have it give of its good treasure to us. He plainly told us to give freely because we had received freely, and this is quite as necessary as is the obeying of any portion of His law.

This is, however, a portion of the universal law that is not as popular in many quarters as it should be; and is, perhaps, one of the reasons why it is so difficult, in many instances, to create the atmosphere of prosperity and plenty. Until we give as graciously and generously as we hope to receive, we have not met the law in this respect, and it is not a law unto us; and, as James says, "Let not that one expect anything of the law."

In passing, I may say that I have had a man send me ten cents, as a free-will offering, and ask me to demonstrate "several million dollars" for his personal use as quickly as possible. And he appeared to think his demand of sufficient importance to attract the attention of the Universal Consciousness and obtain the desired recognition, if only I would be willing to devote ten cents' worth of time to discussing the matter with the Almighty.

Being well aware that even Almighty God was not offering such material trades as that, and not wishing to cheat the man, I returned the ten cents. By this I do not wish to be understood as saying that we are to pay the Almighty in dollars and cents for His great goodness and favor to us. Nothing of the kind. The Universal Law does not so state, and it is by this law that we must be guided, if we would obtain our desires under it. "As ye sow," or as ye give, so also shall ye reap or receive, said our great Teacher. This gives to us an equal opportunity under the law, if we will overcome all selfishness and teach ourselves to love to give, just as much as we love to receive,

This does not shut out from the bounty of Good the one of small means, any more than the one of large means, for in the Scriptures we may read the story of the woman who was able to make but a tiny offering and yet received more of blessing and Spirit recognition than many who gave small fortunes with the hope of obtaining much in return.

We have to learn to trust Spirit with our all, our material things as well as our words, if we would taste its bounty. When we change our longing to get all we can from Spirit to a longing to give all we can, of our time, ourselves and our material things to Spirit and its work, it opens its flood gates of good upon us.

But until we accept the truth that Spirit "knows even the thoughts of our heart" in relation to this matter of giving, as well as of receiving, and so knows when we have earned the right to receive our inheritance, under Father's will, by living precisely as that will prescribes, we shall likely fail in demonstrating that real freedom in our finances that naturally we all long to manifest.

The demonstration of plenty, or of whatsoever we need and desire of material good, rests upon our simple faith in God—the All Power—as our supply, rather than in believing that we must save and hang on to what we have, lest we become impoverished, and have to do without many of the good things of life. To believe that our source of supply must be met from material means of which we have knowledge to-day is not in accord with Christ's teaching as to the manner in which our needs shall be satisfied.

God is our supply, and when we accept Him as such, pouring out our material means as we would have others do for us, if we needed a bit of help, He will manifest in our lives as the richness and fullness of every desire. From many new and unthought of directions His abundance will flow in upon us, and we shall have plenty for every need and selfless desire.

Poverty or lack—and the economy that constantly blossoms into words of what we cannot afford—is quite as much a disease as is rheumatism or the measles, so called, and may and must be cured or healed in precisely the same manner. We must ignore and cast out thoughts and words of lack and fear of poverty, putting in their place thoughts of God as our abundant supply of every good thing, whether physical, mental or material.

When our faith in God is equal to trusting His infinite spirit with any and every thing we have, as the rich young ruler was advised to do, we shall be free, and dollars and cents will mean no more to us than the symbols by which we cheerfully give a fair exchange for what we receive.

Let us think this matter of supply out for ourselves with care and deliberation, and determine to live in accord with the Universal Law as we understand its truth; and if our harvest is not sufficient for every need, it will mean but one thing, namely, that we have arrived at an erroneous interpretation of God's truth and that it will be necessary to obtain a brighter light upon the subject.

Mostly, we talk too much, and think too little. In telling a simple story, or bit of news, too many of us cross and re-cross ourselves, in the matter of language, telling many details which amount to nothing, and repeating, merely by a change of words, many sentences that convey little or no information or knowledge whatsoever.

Were it necessary to pay a penny apiece for the words we use, we would shorten up our stories to the point that they would become far more interesting. But since speech is free, we dissipate or waste words, together with much physical energy, in attempting to prove ourselves ready conversationalists. As a matter of truth, it would be far more economical in many instances were we to pass out our pennies, and conserve our creative energy and force for the purpose for which it was given us.

We can do anything by thought. Thought is all powerful. But this does not mean that we may merely think that a desired thing will come to us while we "serenely fold our hands and wait," and it will do so, minus all further thought and action on our part.

That is not at all in accord with the Universal Law under which we may receive a wonderful inheritance, not only equaling, but far exceeding, all we can ask or even think, if we have first complied with that law and so earned the right to receive our inheritance under it.

Let us not overlook the important fact that there is much for us to do in this matter of creation, about which it will be profitable for us to busy ourselves carefully, until such time as we attract into visibility the thing or condition we desire, and for which we have asked the intercession of All Power.

To state the matter of creating and obtaining our own less plainly, would seem to me to be misleading, and would be to offer a sort of will-o-the-wisp rule by which one might obtain their desired good, or might not, as each experience should prove. The Universal Law operates with precision, and when we have earned the right to receive under it, we shall never be disappointed in our seeking. Until then, it has not become a law unto us, and we do not perfectly trust it.

Apart from the Universal Law we have little to guide us to our All Good, and no real assurance of receiving the desires of our hearts, save as we are able to obtain these things by our own physical and mental force or action. We shall soon discover that merely sitting down and thinking, as optimistically as we are able, that we are going to have an automobile thrust upon us from some unknown source, as a matter of proving to us how simple and admirable is the matter of having all our wants supplied, is hardly a reliable manner in which to provide ourselves with a car if we need to use it upon any specially designated occasion.

To obtain the desires of our hearts—be it an automobile or any lesser or greater thing or condition—we must learn to use our mental realm for the purpose for which it was intended. We must learn to think creative and constructive thoughts. And we must likewise prove by active faith that we "know in Whom we believe," and that we are persuaded that He is both able and willing to do for us all that He has promised.

Active faith means that our acts—the things we do—will indicate and so prove that we have confidence in the system of law by which we work; and that we expect to attract into visibility the things and conditions upon which we have focused our live or creative thought.

For example, we will not merely say we wish we had a certain thing, and that we are going to think we will have it someday, and let it go at that, while we sit with folded hands quoting poetry about the "patient waiter." Should we proceed in that way, we should most likely accomplish nothing, save to perhaps convince ourselves that thought was not as powerful as we like to believe it is.

However, let us remember that hope is not faith; and it is faith, and not hope, that is "the substance of things hoped for: the evidence of things not seen," Paul tells us, and Paul was a very practical and excellent teacher. Faith is the magnet by which we can attract to us even "exceeding, abundantly more than we can even think," if we will first learn to properly exercise our faith by matching it with works.

So let us not merely think we will have a thing desired, at some time and somehow; but rather, let us set about impressing upon the inner mind our need of and desire for the thing. And let us not stop here, but let us ask the inspiration of the Great All Knowledge to give to us the understanding of what, if anything, we are to do further to attract the desired good into visibility in our lives.

The great within—the inner or subconscious mind—does not deal in things. It deals in ideas and it is creative. It will create for us an idea that if accepted with active faith, will attract into sight, from the creative substance all about us, which is God, the specific thing for which we have asked, and which, by our faithful performance of our part of the contract with our Father, we have earned the right to have and receive.

Asking for the things and conditions we desire is only half of the matter. We must grow sufficient faith in the process we are pursuing to listen diligently and expectantly for our answer—the idea; and we must then be quick and alert to run on its errands.

True it is that we can have the desires of our hearts, if we ask as our Father tells us to do—believing that we do receive and believing this sufficiently to listen for the answer, or the idea, which will point out to us the next step. And then let us be ready to take that next step with perfect confidence. For while it is not a new saying that "He who hesitates is lost," it is nevertheless quite a true one and many a time the thing that is put off for a more convenient season is never undertaken and in this way many of our answers to petitions are lost to us.

All Power is Given Unto You

Chapter 11

How to Direct the Mind Dynamo

All Power is Given Unto You

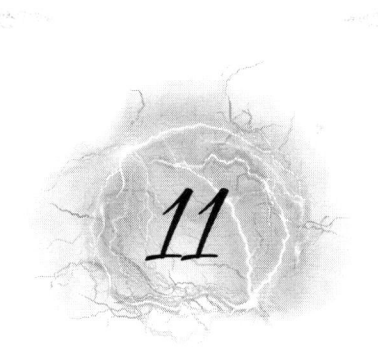

THE world of commerce all about us today owes not a little to the so-called New Thought theory; and while it presents little that is really new, in the way of truth, it offers a sufficiently worth while reward for the business of thinking, individually and originally, to attract the attention of many progressive men and women.

And to those who have faithfully studied and tried out this theory, with the honest expectation of finding the solution of their problems and receiving the satisfaction offered, there have come in many instances wonderfully profitable returns.

Concentrated right thought is daily revolutionizing the world for those who practice it with the expectation of discovering through it the solution of each one of life's problems. This is quite as true when the day's work seems hard and puzzling, as when life appears to run smoothly and well.

The mental realm acknowledges no "Waterloos"; but rather accepts all seeming obstacles with perfect ease and assurance, knowing that the answer is within. It is the outer—the conscious mind only—that fears any test of the inner power. And as fast as the individual understands that all wisdom, knowledge and power is within, he or she likewise knows that a practical application of that power will overcome every seeming difficulty.

And it does.

By calm and concentrated thought, we can unravel all the mysteries of life; since mental application will enable us to learn anything we desire to learn.

Within us is the Power that created the worlds; but before it will create for us the things and conditions we desire, we must learn to use it constructively.

If we really believe in the Power of which we are all individual parts, we shall think well of ourselves; since with that Power all things are possible. Thinking well of ourselves does not mean boasting of what we can do, or what we have. It means recognizing our ancestry, remembering that we are children of Almighty God, the All Good and All Powerful; and so heirs to His wonderful fortune. It means advancement, moving forward toward the things and conditions we desire for our good and for the good of every one of His children, all of which are ours for the asking, if we really believe in the promises of our Elder Brother.

Success of the highest and most satisfying kind comes through acting and achieving. But, underneath the action, must lie the mighty motive power of creative thought: the finest, strongest, most expansive and satisfying substance known to man.

Thought is the world-builder, but it has to build us first. Then it inspires us, if we listen for that inspiration, to build as largely as we are able and willing to conceive.

The world in which we are living, with all its wonderful methods of advancement and progress, is the rich harvest of creative thought of the past and present.

Virgil was really a master of New Thought, but very likely he didn't know it. That he so called himself, we have no record. But of the winning crew in his boat race he said: "They can, because they think they can."

This is the same truth as that uttered by King Solomon, differently expressed. And the same truth being taught today by every so called "Simon pure" New Thought teacher.

Other New Thought masters, who have come down to us across the centuries with their messages of inspiration and helpfulness, are:

- Pythagoras, who lived 600 years before Christ;

- Socrates, the Athenian philosopher;

- Jesus Christ, our Elder Brother, and the great Way-shower in the matter of right living;

- The Apostle Paul, that wonderful teacher and preacher;

- Epictetus and Marcus Aurelius, the Roman emperor;

- As well as scores of others, well known to history because of their "good works, which do follow them."

Each of these renowned teachers presented practically the same truth we are studying and trying to illustrate today, as he understood it individually: the essence of which was and is that love is the greatest thing in the world. And that cheerful, ungrudging and selfless service is love's first and finest fruit; while fear, doubt, resentment and self-seeking are but the advance agents of destruction and disaster.

The progressive thinkers of today are turning back to and teaching this same philosophy of truth—that of love and service—as did those of the earlier days, that right thought, followed by kindly, intelligent and forceful action, will accomplish all things, so gracious is the creative power which is all and in all and which is the motive power within each one of us, ready to come to our aid upon any and every occasion.

Let us determine to take time each day to discuss our problems with the Inner Guide, and to ask for wisdom and understanding, remembering that when we ask, we are to believe that we receive. And let us expect and listen for the help we seek.

When each one of us does this, we shall have found a wonderfully efficient solution for every problem. Even the great problems of so-called capital and labor will melt away like mist before the sun when each one of us recognizes the worthwhileness of being honest and selfless in our seeking. World problems will seem to begin to solve themselves when we, as individuals, stop providing "teeth" for unprofitable controversies.

Elbert Hubbard voiced a great truth when he said that but few of us really think; while the great majority simply think they think, while dealing almost wholly in what he called "Canned Thought," or the product of other minds.

This is a great impediment to both individual and world progress, since it allows a vast amount of the creative power, which is within each individual, to go to waste, in that it produces little that is worthwhile, when each of us might, if he would so determine, learn to use this inner power as our Creator intended us to use it; namely, to bring into visibility in our lives "whatsoever things" we desire.

An original thought, springing up in the mind of an individual, has been the pattern of every great invention the world has known, the benefits of which we are now enjoying. These thoughts or ideas passed from the inner to the outer consciousness, where they were supplemented or supplied with the power of physical action, and they are constantly providing for us a splendid harvest of progress.

But for the all-powerful mental dynamo, combined with the physical activity which it has so ably suggested and superintended, we might still be making our journeys in prairie schooners or on foot, while steamboats, locomotives, telegraph, telephone, electricity, the automobile and airplane, as well as many other wonderful conveniences which we now consider necessities, and without which we could hardly carry on the business of living successfully, would all be unknown—existing only in the creative substance all about us.

The mind is a real dynamo, each of us acting as a "switch" or button which connects or disconnects with all the mental power in existence. If we would keep each individual "switch" workable and healthy, we must know how to properly connect, at all times, with the great All Source of supply; else the "moth and rust" of negative and worthless ideas and imaginings will creep in and defraud us of the realization of our inheritance.

That we can do anything by thought is a simple truth.

But the thought must be intelligent and sustained, and must be followed with the will to do the things suggested by the thought. That is, the thought must be objectified before it will become of real use to us and to the world in which we live.

When we have become masters of our willpower to the extent of doing "whatsoever our hands find to do" as enthusiastically as some of us sit in "cozy corners" building so-called "air castles" under which we never attempt to place an underpinning, then we can truthfully say, as did Napoleon, "There are no Alps." For true it is, "He can who thinks he can."

The world accepts us at the valuation we place upon ourselves. It is our privilege to set up our own standard of personal value, so that if we quit the game of life under the white flag it is our own fault. We have represented ourselves as unequal to our tasks, and "As a man thinketh in his heart, so is he."

The difference between success and failure is very largely a matter of thinking, and the attitude toward life which that thinking suggests. Fix the mental headlight on pictures of success, and success will surely be the harvest. Using "pictures of discouragement and failure in precisely the same manner will just as surely produce a harvest of discontent and dissatisfaction; for the law of creation is unchangeable and unchanging, and results under it can be foretold with precision.

Thoughts are real things, and soon, if indulged, grow into impulses, attracting to themselves strength from many sources; until what began as merely a little casual thought, becomes an irresistible force, blossoming into action, perhaps to greatly enrich and bless the thinker—or, if wrong, to lead, it may be, to untold sorrow and disaster.

There can be no difficulty in our lives, however seemingly great and threatening, that will not be overcome and dissolved by the calm and confident use of the inner power. We are seldom hampered when we know where we are going. It was the old lady who "didn't know where she was going, but was on the way," who found traveling more or less a puzzle.

Let us cultivate constantly the optimistic, kindly and confident attitude of mind, which will set in motion, and keep in continuous operation, those subtle forces which work with us unceasingly to open every door leading to the world's richest treasures.

All Power is Given Unto You

Chapter 12

How to Create and Attract Your Own

All Power is Given Unto You

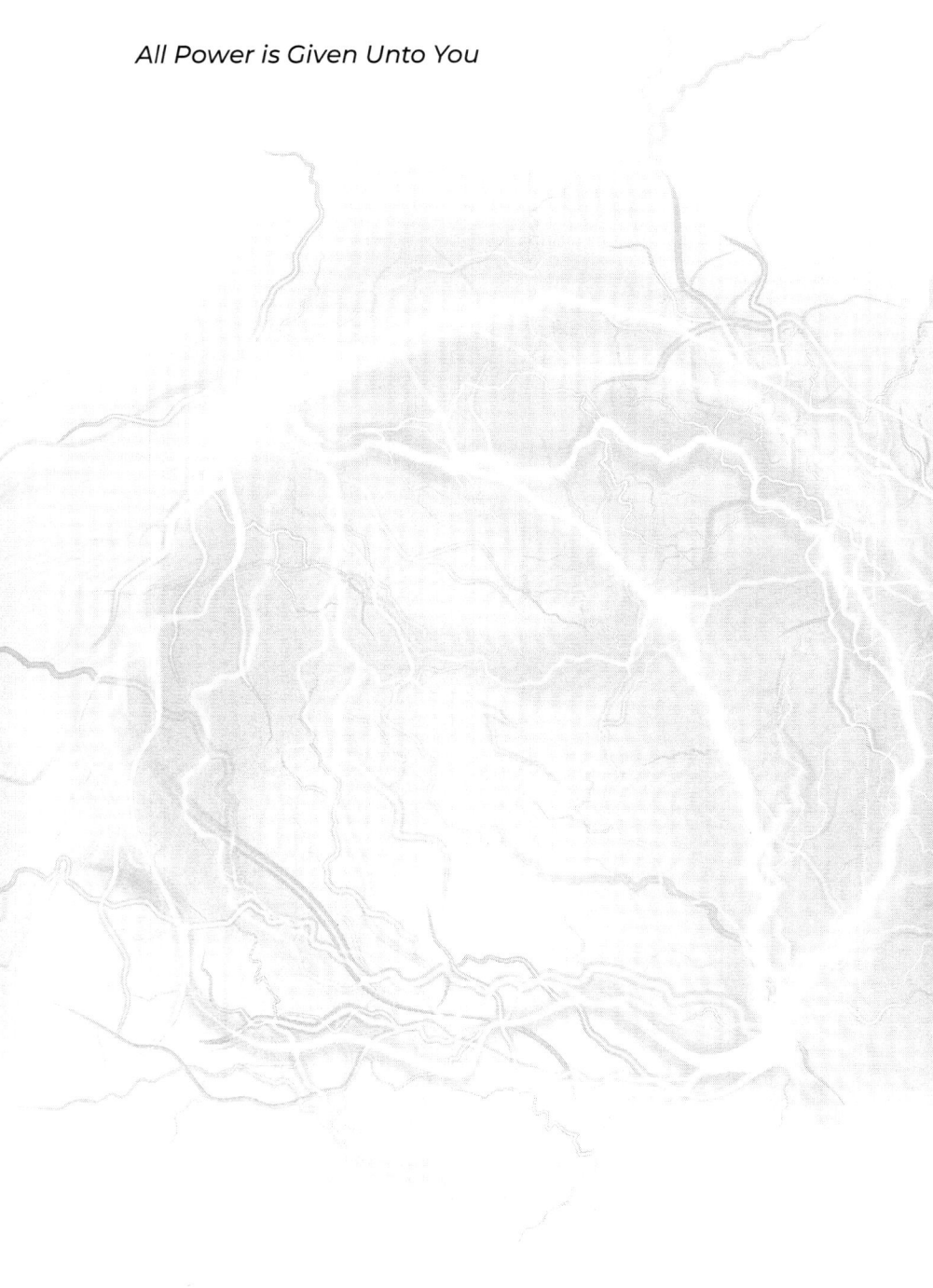

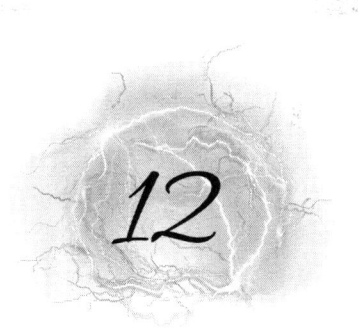

LIFE is not the complex problem many of us have been taught to believe. It is a wonderful experience; each year bringing to us enough of the problematical to keep each individual mind keenly active and alert; that we may create from the substance all about us the things and conditions we are ready to use from day to day for the largest living of which we are capable.

A metaphysical practitioner has recently said that after twenty-five years of experience in this line of work he has learned that there are but few problems of living to be solved; that the seeming complexity comes from the aspect of the individual; that it is complex or interesting, according "as the man thinketh in his heart."

He lists the following questions as those seemingly most puzzling to the people who have sought his aid. It is interesting to note that they are much the same order of inquiries that daily come into our office, with little individual variance.

1. Is it right or proper to ask for and expect to receive a thing one knows of no reasonable way of obtaining?

2. Can one expect to demonstrate a given sum of money—perhaps quite a large amount— at a particular time, when it is desirable to use it?

3. Having asked for some special thing or condition, should one dismiss the matter from the mind, or at each period of silence continue to ask for it?

4. How may one be absolutely sure of obtaining the thing asked for?

5. What is meant by asking amiss?

6. Why do some receive the thing or condition asked for, or sought, instantly, while others, seemingly equally deserving, appear to get no response to their asking?

7. Why is it that one may demonstrate health and yet be unable to accomplish anything in the way of demonstrating supply?

8. Is it a part of God's plan that some remain "poor and in prison"?

9. Should one ask for a thing or condition or affirm that it is already theirs?

10. How can one be sure that the Bible is an inspired book?

11. Will you guarantee to demonstrate for one the thing or condition desired, if they are willing to pay well for such service?

The answer to each of these questions is much the same, if we understand the Universal Law. But many who will read these words do not, else these questions would not so frequently be asked. Because of this I shall try to discuss the questions and answers as I would do with a student personally.

I do not say that my way of interpretation is the only correct one. "The truth shall make you free," said Christ; and that means that each individual may discuss these questions, and all matters coming up for discussion, in accord with the light of knowledge within.

What is truth to me may not yet be truth to another; or he or she may have gone on to some point of seeming greater truth, which makes the lesser seem almost untrue—or at least a weak statement of truth.

So that, if one teacher or interpreter seems to differ from another in his or her manner of presenting the truth, it may be that one has advanced a bit further along certain lines, and so gets a new understanding of the truth; each one presenting truth, from his or her point of inner knowledge.

1.- Before we shall be able to scientifically demonstrate, or manifest, "exceeding, abundantly more than we can ask or even think," we shall have to discover for ourselves what is truth; because it is only the knowledge of truth that makes demonstration a scientific matter.

Apart from truth, we may sometimes succeed, and sometimes fail. But when uncertainty enters into anything in which we are engaged, our house will soon be "divided against itself" and the law tells us that "a house divided against itself cannot stand."

All so-called demonstration, or manifestation, is done after precisely the same law. We create with much accuracy the things and conditions we think about expectantly, whether it is a thing desired or feared.

And by our conversation, or action, we attract these things and conditions into visibility in our lives.

Daily we are given the opportunity to choose a new pattern for our mental work; and if we will do this, choosing such pattern as we desire to live and work in accord with, we may make of ourselves and our surroundings not alone what we today have in mind, but "exceeding, abundantly more than we can ask or even think" today; so generous is our Spirit Father in giving to us the good measure He has promised.

Let us, together, take up the foregoing questions and think on them a bit, since many students seem eager for information along these lines.

To the first question I will say it is proper to ask for, and to confidently expect to receive, a thing that in our limited knowledge we have discovered no way of obtaining. Christ has positively promised that if we ask anything, believing in Him, it shall be done. We cannot get away from that promise, unless we see fit to invalidate all of His Gospel.

Then what is the point of failure? or what is the reason that we do not always receive the thing for which we ask?

We do not believe in Him. And that is our part of the contract. Until we have perfectly complied with this requirement, the promise is of small value to us.

And let us remember that believing means very much more than merely saying that we believe in Christ and His word—or that we believe the Bible, and have so done from childhood. That really means very little in many instances. To say we believe in Him as the Son of God, and as the Christ, and to stop there, is falling far short of the mark.

He expects us to so believe in Him, and His word or law, that we will mark our daily course through life to the letter, and in the spirit, of that law. Anything less than that will mean failure to manifest our desires under its benevolence; since, until we feel it absolutely necessary that we know this law, and obey it implicitly, with cheer and gladness, it is not a law unto us, else we would faithfully study its requirements and determine to fulfill them at all costs.

That we know of no reasonable way of obtaining a thing desired is not a reason why we should desist from asking for it, if we are ready to use that thing for large and worthwhile living. If we ask with faith, believing, that is, expecting to be heard and answered, we shall not be disappointed, unless we disappoint ourselves by failing to do our part.

Failing to listen for Spirit's answer, which answer will tell us how we are to proceed or what we are to do next. It may be to be still and know that the thing for which we ask is ours, right then, at the moment. It may be to do thus or so, for the quickening of our faith. But this listening and obeying the inner inspiration is an important part of the process of manifestation.

2.- It is possible to demonstrate anything we desire, and at a particular time, if necessary, if our faith is equal to the occasion, and if we have earned the right to receive the thing for which we ask. If we have failed to do this, we are unready for the answer to our question. We have been careless of the terms of our contract, and have invalidated it for ourselves. "He that wavers," said James, "is like a wave of the sea, driven and tossed. Let not that one expect anything of the Lord," the Law.

That does not mean that we cannot have the thing or condition we desire; but it does mean that we have not yet earned the right to receive, in accord with His mandate or intention.

3.- Having asked for a special thing, it is not necessary to dismiss the matter wholly from the mind; nor is it necessary to continue to ask or beg for it. It is entirely proper to proceed as we would do if we had asked a loving earthly parent for a favor: expect the granting of our petition, and look forward to the coming of the thing for which we have asked with perfect confidence; willing to await the convenience of the Law, which works in devious and wonderful ways its errands to perform, but never fails to fulfill to the uttermost each one of its promises and missions.

4.- We may be assured of attracting to ourselves the thing or condition upon which we mentally dwell, or expectantly think. Mind is an individual creator within each one of us, and as we think, so we are—or so do we create for ourselves.

When we appear not to manifest (or receive) the thing or condition desired and sought for, or something "exceeding, abundantly better" than we have asked or even thought, it is because we have dissipated our mental force, or have allowed it to fluctuate. We have thought for a little on the things desired, and then have speculated on what could be done if the things desired did not materialize, or become visible and usable.

Thus we have divided our mental house against itself, setting up first a positive and then a negative pole; attracting by our faith in the thing desired, and repelling, just as naturally, by our doubts and fears.

Both states of consciousness are creative, and create after their kind, and cannot create in any other manner. It must always be a matter of "According to thy faith, be it unto thee." If our real faith is in All Good, our creations or manifestations will be good; while if our faith is in things we fear, and about which we worry, our manifestations are quite sure to follow along in that line, with very much of accuracy, under the same universal law of consciousness.

5.- We ask amiss when we ask or affirm in any other way than as directed by our Elder Brother, whose needs and desires were much the same as ours. He solved His problems by perfect laws, by which we can likewise solve ours. His mission, here upon the earth, was to demonstrate to us how life's problems may be mastered, if we will determine to know the truth, and then at all times live that knowledge with confidence.

We likewise ask amiss when we ask God to do for us the things it is our business to do for ourselves. To actively engage in our affairs is not His business. And yet, how frequently we beg of Him to really do for us the unpleasant or difficult duty, seeming to expect Him to do it while we sit comfortably down, with folded hands, so to speak, inactive, both physically and mentally.

Universal Mind deals with ideas, not with materials. It is full of patterns, from which we may select our own, and by it, and with the help of All Mind, fashion for ourselves "all things, whatsoever we desire." But when we ask God, or Infinite Spirit, to put into our hands the things we desire, without any exhibition of faith on our part, other than our saying that we believe with God all things are possible, we ask amiss; and in most instances we shall be reminded of His "Ye ask, and receive not, because ye ask amiss"—or without fulfilling His law, and so earning the right to have the thing or condition we desire.

His work in our behalf was done some thousands of years ago, and when we believe this, and live up to the conditions of His centuries-old law, our faith and works combined in agreement will act as a magnet, attracting into sight, from the creative substance all about us, the things and conditions we desire. Yes, we can always have the things we desire, and for which we have a right use. But these things will not drop from the clouds into our arms merely for the asking—or praying—as some of us are seemingly prone to expect, or at least hope.

God's ideas, patterns, thoughts, if you please, will come to us as often as we seek them honestly. And we really need nothing more; for with His ideas coming to us as inspiration, we are the architects of our own fortune. We may ask whatsoever we will, and from His creative substance all about us, if we will hold constantly to our pattern with confidence, we may be sure of creating for ourselves the desired good.

And the things and conditions we create, under this law, are ours and no other force can take them from us, until we are done with them; or until we are ready to exchange, or replace them, with something better, which Spirit has for us, and of which it reminds us, by pushing a new thought, or desire, into the individual mind, which new thought, if fostered and encouraged, soon becomes a reality, taking the place of the former thing or condition with which we are done; it having served its purpose in our lives.

All Knowledge does not need to study our petitions for the purpose of reaching a decision as to whether or not the thing for which we ask would be best for us.

Had this been the intent of Spirit in the beginning we would not have the promise, "And if ye ask anything, in My name, I will do it." Theology has misinterpreted His "Thy will, not mine, be done," it would seem; and the will of God is, that we may have "exceeding, abundantly above what we can ask or even think," at any moment when we have earned the right to so receive, by living in accord with Universal Law.

He has not made of us automatons, to do precisely as He directs. But rather, having told us what and how to live, He has made us free agents to obey His law, or not to obey it, as we will. But it is only by obeying and living in accord with this law that we can obtain its benefits. Failing to do this, James indicates what is likely to be our portion, in his "Let not that one expect anything of the Lord."

The matter is really in our own hands, and we may profit or not, as we choose. But until we ask aright, that is, until we have sufficient respect for His law to determine to know its requirements and fulfill them to the letter, our petitions are likely to be largely in vain, and to bring to us little in the way of satisfaction; since we have not made His law a law unto us. But, we have seemingly expected the great Law Maker to so change His law that it will accommodate our wishes, if it be His will.

6.- Having asked for the thing we desire, let us affirm thereafter that we have received, that the thing is ours; and if we will steadfastly and confidently believe ourselves—our affirmation—this believing will be the magnet that will attract into sight the thing claimed, in accord with the promise, "When ye ask, believe that ye receive, and ye shall have."

It hardly seems necessary to continue to ask for

the desired good under this positive promise. It is better to give thanks to the Father mind, that we have been heard and answered, and that the thing desired is ours. It is, in Spirit's knowledge, even before we ask. And from Spirit has come to the individual mind the desire—a sort of forerunner of its bounty.

This agreeing, or gracious state of mind, if continued with faith, will create for us, and attract into sight, the thing or condition we seek. And it will likely appear in our lives from some perfectly natural source, for All Power seldom works supernaturally. All is God—or Good—and from whatsoever source our desired good comes to us, it comes from God. God is the only Presence and the only Power, and there is no other source from which we can hope to obtain.

7.- Instant healing comes when our faith is simple and honest, and when we hold the mind firmly and steadily to the condition desired, rather than to allow ourselves to judge by appearances. Healing comes through the mind of Christ, which is within each one of us, if we will teach ourselves to rise to that attitude of mind and accept it in truth, both mentally and materially or physically.

It matters not how we look, feel or appear. If we will recall the promises of Christ, and accept them as just as possible in our individual cases as they were in the time when He walked upon the earth, we shall be made every whit whole; and we need give no heed to any lesser authority, no matter how reasonable or probable it may be made to appear.

The woman whose faith caused her to press through the crowd to touch the hem of Christ's garment was made every whit whole instantly, and for all time. Similar faith, on the part of any individual, would be likewise rewarded; but "without faith, it is impossible to please God," we are told.

Too often we do our reasoning as to these things on the negative side. For a moment we seem to have faith, and inspiration tries to direct us to the desired good. Then we begin to argue within ourselves, "Yes, I might get the thing (or healing) desired. But suppose I did not." This woman might have mentally said, "This is a terrible crowd. I don't believe I could make my way through it anyway, and I'll wait until some time when it will be easier." Suppose you that that would have instantly healed her trouble?

Of course it would not. But apparently doubts and fears had no place in her mind. She was intent upon making her way through the crowd, regardless of difficulty. She did the thing inspiration suggested to her. She had the living faith that to touch even the hem of His garment would be all-sufficient for her need. She didn't merely sit and beg for health, and fear she would not be heard, or, if heard, that she might not be answered in accord with her desire. But she did the thing her mind (the God power within her) told her to do, regardless of all that stood between her and the Christ man that made the doing seem difficult.

Was the result any different than would be the result in your life or mine, if we, upon all occasions, did the thing the inner mind told us to do, and did it expecting the result promised? Not a particle. When our faith and works agree, and when they meet the universal law of asking and receiving, that law will always operate unerringly in our behalf.

The physical act of touching the hem of Christ's garment, of course, had nothing to do with the healing. The healing came through the perfect faith of the woman, as proven by her works. And Spirit, which knows even the thoughts of our hearts, knows when we trust the All Good and when we distrust it and really believe only those things which are apparent to the physical senses.

8.- It is true there are many who appear to demonstrate health, but seem unable to manifest material wealth, or supply. The explanation of this state of affairs is not as difficult, however, as many apparently think it. All demonstration is a matter of creation. And we must create for ourselves the things and conditions we desire before we can take possession of them.

It seems difficult to convince a good many people that the supply of all and every good thing is ample for every individual, if that individual will so believe, and honestly live that belief as freely and fearlessly as a child lives in the bosom of its family, without a thought of worry as to where his daily supply is to be obtained.

The child does not eat a little of what is given him and determine to "lay up," or "save," as much of it as possible, for a "rainy day." No, he enjoys to the full the good that is within his reach, leaving the "rainy day," and all other days, to be cared for in turn, as they come along, by the power having dominion over him. Like trust in the power having dominion over us would bring into operation in our lives a law of supply that is ample for every need; and not only ample, but "exceeding, abundantly above all we can ask or even think" in its supplying possibilities.

There is a perfect law of prosperity, if we will

take the trouble to study and understand it. It is not wholly a matter of getting, clinging, having, saving for ourselves. It is largely a matter of giving, as we desire and wish to receive. A planting, as it were, of the prosperity seed; knowing that as we sow, we may be absolutely sure of reaping.

Paul says, "If ye sow sparingly, ye shall reap also sparingly; and if ye sow bountifully, ye shall reap also bountifully. Every man, as he purposeth in his heart, so let him give; not grudgingly, or of necessity, for God loveth a cheerful giver."

That is a wonderfully wise explanation of the prospering law of Universal Mind. "And God is able to make all grace abound toward you; that ye, always having all sufficiency in all things, may abound to every good work."

We have to get away, for all time, from the economy thought which has been fostered all down the ages and change the mind to the other side of the question, that of giving, giving, giving all that we feel it is right to give in order to really help the world's work. Giving as we would like another to give for us, under similar conditions, if we needed a little material lift.

We need to realize that money is but the symbol of doing something worthwhile; rather than merely a wall between us and the so-called poorhouse. Let us free it, and let it go, blessing it as it goes, and inviting it to return, bringing with it the "good measure, pressed down, shaken together and running over" He has promised to such as believe in Him sufficiently to do any and every thing He suggests.

It is the habit of clinging to our money, disliking to spend it freely and graciously, that shuts off the material supply. Until we really trust God with our dollars, just as willingly as we trust Him with our "much speaking," we shall very likely find that we have failed in the "one point," that James tells us may hold us "guilty of all." This is where most of us fail in demonstrating material supply.

"As a man thinketh in his heart, so is he." And if we think our supply is a little money which we have placed in bank or in bond, so it is unto us. And we have shut off the great universal flow of All that we can ask or even think as a reality in our lives.

In truth, God is our supply, in every department of our lives; and God is equal to our every need. God is our health, our wealth, our happiness, our All and in all, if we will only so believe and receive. The very day that we decide to trust Him with all we have, we shall likewise realize that we have found the open road to prosperity. His inspiration will speak to us constantly, teaching us to create for ourselves the things and conditions that today seem far beyond our reach.

Faith is the magnet that attracts into sight material good, precisely as it attracts into sight all things for which we ask, believing.

The same law by which we demonstrate health will just as surely and accurately demonstrate material supply. In every instance it is a matter of trusting God, the All Good, fully and freely, and looking not to material things as the cause of our desired good fortune.

If we will put the matter of receiving upon an honest business basis, and expect only such return as we have earned the right to receive, we shall not be disappointed; and we shall soon become familiar with the prospering law.

Until we do this, this law has not become a law unto us, and we have few rights under it. It is not a matter of "As ye reap, so are ye to sow," or give of your good. That is not what He has promised. And when we turn this law about in that way we completely invalidate it in our behalf.

Spirit does not promise to trust us; and it does make it a matter of importance that we trust

Him. If we were to receive all His benefits first, and then do our giving, no faith in God would be required. It would be merely a matter of His trusting us to be fair with Him.

But Universal Law makes all these matters tests of our real faith in it, first promising us that "According to our faith it is unto us." And until we have faith we are nothing, so far as creating and attracting into sight from Spirit substance goes. If we give nothing, or "give grudgingly" what we do offer, let us remember that we have only earned the right to receive in like manner; and that by giving a few pennies we have no right to expect the return of a fortune.

Anyone who is failing in the matter of demonstrating supply will find the cause (of which the failure is the effect), if they will study carefully and honestly the law of compensation recited by Christ, and further discussed by Paul, for the benefit of the people he taught so successfully. We must know the truth as to the matter of giving, and live that knowledge before we shall have really established our right to receive.

When we do this, we shall have no reason whatsoever to complain of Spirit's generosity in our behalf. It will at all times operate for us, as "exceeding, abundantly more than we can ask or even think," for the largest living of which we are mentally capable.

Illness, unhappiness, lack, disharmony of every degree are effects of wrong or destructive thinking and living. Change the thought method, even though it costs some sacrifice, mentally, physically or materially, and plenty will flow into your life like a beautiful river, bringing to you daily sufficient for every need, as naturally as night follows the day.

This does not mean that money will drop from the clouds into our hands, but rather, that All Mind will operate through us, as an idea or inspiration which we may accept, and promote to the greatest success of which we are capable of thinking, if we will see to it that our faith is followed by the necessary works. But faith without works is as dead now as was the case in the time of Paul, let us remember.

9.- No, assuredly it is never a part of God's plan that one of His children remain any different from every other one of His family. "Ask what ye will, believing in Me, and it shall be done," and "If ye ask anything in My name, I will do it," are positive promises, made to one of God's children just as much as to another; and both are so simple and straightforward that it would seem as though even he who runs might read in them His truth.

It is the truth that makes us free. But merely knowing the truth will not be sufficient. We may know the truth ever so well, and fail to live in accord with its teaching, and we shall not be satisfied. It is when we cooperate with truth, even in the smallest particular, that we feel its benefits, and know that all bondage is a thing of the past.

10.- To the one who is not sure that the Bible is an inspired book, it is a rather thankless task to prove that it is; for "As a man thinketh in his heart, so is he." And if one thinks the Bible is not inspired, he will hardly draw much inspiration from it. I would answer the question by saying that it is not a matter of great importance, as I see it, whether it is inspired or not. Perhaps in the past creeds have given too much time to discussions of that, and similar phases of inquiry; have laid more stress on the "was inspired" than upon the present "does inspire."

A perfectly satisfactory disposal of this question to me is that the Bible inspires me, as I read its record of those who have gone before. As I read the Gospels I feel the truth of that wonderfully inspiring sentence, "There is a spirit in man, and the inspiration of the Almighty giveth him understanding"; and I say it is enough.

That inspiration constantly comes to my aid and so enlightens my understanding that I seem to see and feel the Christ at my side, pointing out to me, so simply and perfectly, the truth I seek—the answer to my problem, printed there, it may be, in Christ's words. And again I say, I am satisfied.

This Gospel inspires me to go forward and onward, with my face constantly toward His promise, "He that believeth on Me, the works that I do, shall he do also; and greater works than these shall he do."

11.- No teacher or practitioner could well guarantee to demonstrate even a dime for another; for it is now precisely as it was in the time when Christ walked upon the earth. And to each one coming to Him for healing, or for whatever seeming miracle, He said, "Thy faith hath made thee whole"; and, again, "Without faith ye are nothing."

A teacher or practitioner can point the way; can act as a lamp to the feet, as it were, to hasten the growth of faith, but cannot have faith for the one who is lacking in that particular need. "When ye ask, believe that ye receive, and ye shall have," is the promise. And until we have faith; until we believe that we have received the good thing or condition desired, we are nothing so far as Universal Consciousness is concerned with our petition, since we have not earned the right to its recognition.

"Faith," said Paul, "is the substance of things hoped for—the evidence of things not seen." Faith, then, is the body of our desired good. It is the magnet that shall attract that good into visibility, and out of the creative substance from which all things are made. Faith speaks within us, to tell us that the desired good exists for us, and is awaiting our attracting power; and "according to our faith, it is unto us" in every instance.

If we really believe the Universal Law, we must receive "whatsoever we desire" under it. But there is no formula, or combination of words, by the simple use of which one may expect to demonstrate even a nickel, let alone several million dollars, as has been suggested to me many times by someone who had no more pronounced need of the money than to see how it felt to be rich.

It is faith in God—the All Good, the Great Source of All—that is the creative power and that can always be depended upon to create for us as we will. And let us remember that creating "our own" does not mean that we can think first trustingly and then doubtingly, and still create only the things in which we delight. "Our own" is the thing or condition with which we mentally connect or relate ourselves, whether it be with faith in good or fear of ill or so-called evil. As we think, so shall we create for ourselves; and whatsoever we create is "our own," and will be attracted into visibility in our lives. So let us see to it that we think aright.

Demonstration or manifestation is wholly a matter of knowing the universal law of truth, and meeting the demands of that law to the letter and in the spirit. Merely to "hold the thought," "God is my supply," for twenty minutes or half an hour, and then to arise and go about, proving by the words we utter and the acts we perform that we do not believe the word of truth we have affirmed, accomplishes nothing for us. Nor can a teacher or practitioner attract into the life of another anything that that other has not perfectly earned the right to receive.

When we speak the creative word, following it up with the natural action which indicates that our faith and works agree, we shall have no occasion to question our ability to demonstrate whatsoever we desire; for demonstration is only the Absolute engaged in its natural and perfect work.

The complete theory of demonstrating or manifesting the things and conditions we desire is contained in Matthew's record of the teaching of Christ, beginning with the twenty-fifth verse of the sixth chapter. In the next to the last verse Christ said: "But seek ye first the Kingdom of God and His righteousness (rightness), and all these things (meaning the things we shall eat, the things we shall drink, and wherewithal we shall be clothed, as related earlier in the chapter) shall be added unto you."

If we will put aside less important matters and honestly and faithfully give our attention to seeking His Kingdom of Good within ourselves, which will inspire us to do by others as we would like them to do by us, we shall very soon find ourselves at the goal of satisfaction.

For the inner mind is both willing and able to create for us all and everything for which the outer, or conscious mind, will furnish a pattern.

How to Create and Attract Your Own - 12